SCRIPTURES, SECTS AND VISIONS

SCRIPTURES, SECTS
AND VISIONS

A Profile of Judaism from Ezra to the Jewish Revolts

MICHAEL EDWARD STONE

Associate Professor
Institute of Jewish Thought
Hebrew University of Jerusalem

FORTRESS PRESS
Philadelphia

Published by
Collins

Cleveland   New York   London   Glasgow
Toronto   Sydney   Auckland   Johannesburg
and by
Maitland Publications Pty. Ltd.
88 Brighton St., Petersham
N.S.W. 2049

First published in the U.S.A. 1980
Library of Congress Catalog Card Number 79-54151
U.S. ISBN 0-529-05722-5

First published in Great Britain 1980
U.K. ISBN 0 00 215051 4

Set in Baskerville and Printed in Australia by Hogbin, Poole (Printers) Pty. Ltd., Sydney.

To My Parents

RECA AND JULIUS STONE

Who Taught Me to Love the Search
for Understanding

ACKNOWLEDGEMENTS

This book has its genesis as a series of six lectures delivered in the spring of 1978 to K.A.M. Isaiah Israel Congregation in Hyde Park, Illinois, as a Scholar-in-Residence under the aegis of the Jacob J. Weinstein Memorial Fund established by the family of the late Jacob Levin. Rabbis Simeon J. Maslin and Hayim G. Perlmutter both showed great kindness to me at that time and encouraged me, as did my friend, Professor Joseph Kitagawa of the University of Chicago Divinity School. The impetus to expand and rewrite them as a book came from my father, Julius Stone, to whom I am indebted for so much, and this too. Such debts can never be repaid; they are gladly acknowledged.

The book was written while I was a guest at Ormond College in the University of Melbourne, on the kind invitation of its Master, J. Davis McCaughey. That stay was another of the many benefits the College and its wise Master have over the years afforded me.

J. Davis McCaughey and Peter Mitchell read the book in manuscript and made many helpful comments indeed. Any errors of fact and judgement are, of course, my own.

MICHAEL E. STONE

Hebrew University of Jerusalem
January, 1980.

*　　　*　　　*　　　*　　　*

PREFACE

It seems appropriate to open this book by saying what it is not. It is not a systematic introduction to the history of the literature and religion of Judaism in the period of the Second

vii

Temple. Neither is this a book primarily for scholars and technical experts, although one hopes that they will find some points of interest in it, or something they wish to dispute. This book does not set out to present its subject from the viewpoints of biblical studies or rabbinics; students of those disciplines, nonetheless, may find its change of perspective instructive.

Instead, it is a somewhat idiosyncratic presentation of some of the things that I have found surprising in my recent studies of the history of Judaism in the Second Temple period. Certain of these surprises were so great as to change my view of what Judaism looked like then, of what it was, and how it developed. Others were not so revolutionary, but still forced me to stop, reconsider and evaluate anew positions and ideas about the past that I had held for years. If I can succeed in communicating some of that surprise and its implications, I shall have succeeded in what I set out to do.

This particular segment of the past has been important to men whose culture is informed by Judaism or Christianity, that is, to peoples of Western civilization. New perceptions and new understanding are significant and need to be worked out in detail, and that is the task I have here undertaken. This is not the place to present technical arguments or scientific descriptions of new discoveries, but to try to see how the implications of those arguments and those discoveries impinge upon our perception of the realities of an ancient day. So I have dispensed with the scholar's apparatus of footnotes, preferring to supply a bibliography at the end of the book. This will serve to indicate the work of my predecessors upon which I have drawn freely, and also some directions of reading which the interested reader might wish to pursue. I have also added an alphabetic list of all ancient writings mentioned, providing some general details about them for the convenience of the reader.

M.E.S.

January, 1980

Contents

1

THE ENTERPRISE

There are periods of history as there are places on earth which seem to have been particularly important for the development of the religious and intellectual culture in which we live. Fifth century Athens was one such; Italy at the time of the Renaissance was another; a third was the eastern Mediterranean basin in the last pre-Christian centuries and the early years of the present era. We shall try here to gain some insights into that particular age and that particular place.

The great events that took place then and there were the beginning and spread of Christianity and the development of Rabbinic Judaism. So, one might ask, why should these events be studied again? Has not the devotion of two thousand years' diligent labour taught us almost all that there is to know about them? Is there not a consensus, accepted by most scholars, on what happened then and how it all developed?

The fact of the matter is that modern man has a great deal to learn from a re-examination of that time and that place. Events do not happen in a vacuum; to understand them one must know the context in which they came about. When the time of those events and the place in which they happened are examined, they turn out to be singularly interesting.

The Jews lived in the hill country of Judea, while the Egyptians and the Babylonians inhabited the fertile valleys of the Nile and the Land between the Two Rivers. The Egyptians and the Babylonians had a culture millennia old, so old that by the middle of the first millennium B.C.E. some of them had developed an antiquarian interest in their own past. Jewish culture was younger—the Jews had entered the land of Canaan some time around 1200 B.C.E., and by the end of the last pre-Christian millennium they had developed a strong and vigorous civilization. They had never held political power, except for some brief interludes such as the age of David and Solomon. Such power had always been the prerogative of the rulers of the Nile valley or of the Land between the Two Rivers, and the Jewish kingdoms existed only as reflections of the weakness of these. At a later time the Persians constituted yet one further factor in the complex of ancient Near Eastern civilizations. This Indo-European people originated beyond Mesopotamia, although they assimilated many elements of its culture after they conquered Babylon in 539 B.C.E. There were features of their own culture and administration which were new, however, and were to prove important for future developments in the area. (See below, Chapter 2.)

So, one set of elements in this world of the turn of the eras which we are setting out to describe was the age-old cultures of the Near East. Another element, and a central one, was the Greeks. Philip of Macedon had united the perpetually fractious city-states which dotted the Greek peninsula. His son Alexander had conquered the east; what is crucial for us is not just that he conquered the east, but that he Hellenized it. He undertook a systematic policy, which was furthered by his successors, designed to implant Greek culture throughout the empire he had taken for himself. Throughout this, the largest empire the world had yet seen, Greek cities and colonies were established and Greek culture spread from Sogdia and Bactria in the east to Marseilles and the western Mediterranean.

The great flowering of classical Greek culture was, as every schoolboy once knew, in Athens in the fifth century B.C.E. The age of Pericles, the writings of the great dramatists, the philosophy of Plato, the building of the Acropolis—these were among its achievements. But Athens in that century was an independent city-state, as were the other cities of Greece. In many ways, in such cities, people's political, social and intellectual vision was bounded by the borders of their city. When Philip united Greece and Alexander built his empire, the horizons of Greece suddenly widened, the walls of the city-state were cast down. The availability of the east must have had an impact on the Greeks analogous to that of the discovery of the New World upon Europe. But, unlike what the Europeans experienced in the Americas, in the east the Greeks encountered ancient and highly sophisticated cultures, by which, in the end, they were deeply influenced.

The story of the period that follows, the so-called Hellenistic age, is partly the story of how the cultures of the Greeks and of the orient interacted and fused. The kingdoms into which Alexander's empire was divided within decades of his death in 323 B.C.E. needed Greeks as soldiers, administrators and settlers. And the Greeks came in large numbers, encouraged by the conditions in Greece and by the incentives laid before them by the Hellenistic rulers. They established cities after their own fashion and set up the institutions of culture and education which were the basis and hallmark of their way of life. These were common throughout the world of the Hellenistic kingdoms. A man could move from one end of that world to the other and find Greek culture, Greek institutions and familiar patterns of life and society.

Yet there were factors which gradually modified this dominant Greek culture. One was that the term "Hellene" or Greek came to designate men who were Greek by culture, not necessarily by tribal or ethnic origin. Such men were accepted as citizens of the new cities. Thus, the dominant culture became available to people of oriental descent, and many of the leading lights of Greek thought and culture throughout the Hellenistic period were orientals by origin. The Stoic school of philosophy developed in the Hellenistic period and was one of the most influential intellectual movements in late antiquity. Zeno, the first great figure of Stoicism, was an oriental; he came from the coast of Syria (modern Lebanon) and it is related of him that he spoke Greek with a foreign accent to the end of his life. His is not an isolated instance. At a different level of interchange, there was a growing measure of contact and inter-marriage between the Greek settlers and the native orientals as the Greek settlements persisted into the second and third generation and longer. Moreover, there was always the contact of the market-place.

In spite of all this, throughout much of the east there were large areas in which the native culture remained unchanged and even flourished. Indeed, many of the orientals nurtured a healthy dislike of Greek domination, as later they resented the Romans. Alexander of Macedon founded a city on the Nile Delta which became the centre of the Greek east. In the great metropolis of Alexandria in the first century, in addition to the self-governing Greek city, there were large quarters inhabited by Syrians, Jews and other foreigners. The royal court and administration of the Ptolemies, too, although situated in Alexandria, were not part of the Greek city of Alexandria. In the hinterland of Egypt, as elsewhere in the east, the life of the villages must have continued unchanged.

Clearly, then, the world was now a far more complex place than it had been in the fifth or even in the fourth century in Athens or Corinth. The cult of the gods had been intimately tied into the civic life. With the uprooting of family and tribal ties and the establishment of new cities, this city cult no longer satisfied the needs of men. Instead, Greek religion and philosophy underwent a metamorphosis in which oriental elements played an ever-increasing role. This metamorphosis has been described as the development of personal religion. In the new forms of religion and religious philosophy, men faced by a much larger and more complex world sought to find solace, confidence and a role in society. The new forms of religion were often characterized by devotion to a specific personal deity and were frequently carried on in *thiasoi* or private asssociations. These were sometimes mere monthly dining clubs, but often they were devoted to the veneration of a particular deity. This process of change was accentuated by another feature of Hellenistic religion. Polytheism had always been syncretistic, tending to identify with one another deities who seemed to share similar features, even though they were worshipped in different lands or cities. This tendency gathered increasing impetus in the Hellenistic age as men moved in the broad world which Alexander's conquests had created. The Greeks called the deities of the eastern peoples by Greek names and identified them with their own gods. They interpreted the myths of the orient in Greek terms. Such syncretistic identification, however, did not utterly change the character of the oriental god. Instead, it enabled his integration into the Greek view of the world.

Cults developed in the Hellenistic period which were centred around such oriental deities. They frequently promised their adherents salvation or illumination, to be gained by a series of revelations and initiations: these were the so-called mystery religions. Such deities as Isis, the Egyptian goddess of wisdom, became the centre of widely diffused Hellenized cults of this type, and there were quite a number of others.

Parallel with this development, there was a growing number of attempts by the intellectuals of the oriental cultures to write about and interpret their religion and traditions in Greek. This process reflected in part the grappling of the mythopoeic oriental way of thinking with the systematic, philosophical reasoning introduced by the Greeks. The orientals' natural desire to present their own culture and past in terms which were comprehensible to the dominant and challenging Greek culture must also have played a part in it. So, many eastern religions developed theories or theologies at this time, and did so in the Greek language. Manetho, the Egyptian priest who counselled the first Ptolemy on native Egyptian religion, wrote a work on Egyptian culture and history in Greek. Another such oriental was Berossus the Babylonian; a third was Philo Byblus of Phoenicia.

Certain eastern religious ideas and views gained great vogue in the Greek-speaking world. From the time of Herodotus (sixth century) on, the Greeks had tended to idealize the learning of the east, seeking to find in it the secrets of true piety and wisdom. This veneration of oriental saints and wise men and their teachings continued and indeed gathered force as men sought for forms of religion outside the traditional cults of Greece. One expression of it was in the spread of astrology. This "science" had been developed in Mesopotamia; it was provided with a theoretical structure in the Hellenistic age, and its practitioners became known as *Chaldaioi* or "Chaldeans" (originally the name of an ethnic group in Mesopotamia). Astrological belief was particularly well suited to certain themes of the Hellenistic view of the world, for it demanded that man accept a fate fixed by the stars. This removed him from the tensions which complexities of life in the Hellenistic world imposed.

By the second pre-Christian century, then, a shift was taking place in the world of thought. One main theme of it was a deepening sense of alienation. Men felt themselves to be out of tune with the world. They sought the assurance of religious or philosophical systems which would remove them from this quandary. At its most extreme, the feeling of alienation led to the view that man did not really belong in the world at all, but beyond it or outside it. Since the sixth or fifth century B.C.E., the idea had been around that man was composed of two parts, body and soul, and that the body constrained or weighed down the soul. This idea was pithily expressed by the famous word play *sōma* = *sēma* ("body = grave"). The dualism thus epitomized contributed to the growing sense of alienation which men had. Body and world became bound together and the purpose of religion and of many religious philosophies became to find a way of assuring the release of the soul or spirit from the "tomb" of the body or the world. Various forms of Hellenistic religion drew much from older Greek ideas, but many of them were equally deeply indebted to oriental views and cults, often in their *interpretatio graeca* or syncretistic form.

Such are, then, in brief outline, some of the chief characteristics of the Hellenistic religious spirit. It should be stressed, of course, that the growth in popular religion and oriental cults in no way affected the conduct of the civic cult in the Greek cities. Their founding and tutelary deities continued to receive official worship, just as the imperial cult persisted unchanged, later on, in the Roman empire. Moreover, the intellectual range and creativity of Hellenistic learning, science and medicine were extraordinary in a multitude of fields of human endeavour. Yet, those features we have mentioned seem to be particularly prominent among the characteristics of Hellenistic religious life and thought.

By the second pre-Christian century the expansion of Rome towards the east was under way, and the political history of the area is the story of the inexorable advance of Rome, until stopped at the farther reaches of the Seleucid realm by the newly-constituted Parthian monarchy. But Roman hegemony did not lead to a Latinization of the cultural and religious life of the east. Changes did take place, chiefly under the Empire, but they were changes within the Greek-speaking east itself. Alexander's policy of Hellenization was successful, then, and by a century or two after his death a uniform Greek culture had been established throughout the east: not a purely Greek culture, of course, but in some ways a synthesis of Greek and oriental elements. This Graeco-oriental culture was and remained distinguishable from the Latin-speaking culture which was developing in the west. The cultural division was perpetuated in later centuries in the divided Roman empire with its centres at Byzantium and Rome. In our own day we see the differences perpetuated in the contrast between the western churches with their Latin background and the eastern (i.e. Greek) churches with their roots deep in the culture of eastern Europe and of the ancient oriental world of the Near East.

The Near East became the Greek-speaking world as a direct result of Alexander's policies, and this was the world in which Judaism lived and developed and changed. Two directions must be traced in this development. One, the "vertical" axis, goes back into the preceding centuries, and along it one can perceive the cultural givens of Judaism and how they changed and persisted. The other, the "horizontal" axis, is that of the general movements of religious thought, the *Zeitgeist* of the Hellenistic age in which at this time Judaism lived.

In some ways, the situation was rather like the present one. Traditional patterns of religious belief and conduct no longer determine much of that range of human thought and action which they did a few generations ago. Men seek to find faiths or beliefs by which they may order their lives in an increasingly complex world. One response to this situation is a growth of superstition and irrationalism. Even that attitude towards the orient and its wisdom as endowed with special profundity has been widespread in some western countries; strange cults seem to have found footholds and followings. Some of them are developments of religious patterns already existing in the society. Others are imported from outside the western cultural area and are adapted to some extent to the needs of western culture. One should avoid, of course, drawing such analogies in too rigorous a fashion, but intriguing parallels do exist.

In the history of Judaism, too, the similarities between the modern situation and that of Judaism in the Hellenistic age are noteworthy. Judaism is trying (and has been doing so since the emancipation of western European Jewry) to find its balance within and over against the broader cultural context. The experiments in this have run all the way from assimilation to pietistic separatism. It is, however, the attempts at meeting and synthesis that show the most striking similarities with the Hellenistic age, though at that time there were also highly assimilated Jews. Philosophical interpretations of Judaism in the terms of prevailing intellectual fashions are one form of such attempts. Another striking parallel between the Hellenistic period and the present is that an independent Jewish State now exists for the first time since the subjugation of the Hasmonean monarchy to Rome. Judaism, for the first time in two millennia, is developing as the majority culture of an independent Jewish State. The Hellenistic age is the last time this happened. The analogies are many, but so are the differences, and facile inferences from the past should be avoided. Yet there may be something to learn for the present situation from that of the Hellenistic age, and from attention to the overall context in which Judaism flourished and developed then.

The description given here of the origins and growth of Hellenistic culture and religion has been familiar for some time. Now, however, we need to look at it again, and to re-examine how Judaism developed in the Hellenistic world. The writing of history is a process of interpretation, and history must be written anew by each generation. This is partly because each generation looks at it in a different perspective, and partly because new evidence becomes available. In recent decades new sources for the study of the period that concerns us have emerged, and these new sources demand changes in the way we describe the events, and they illuminate previously dark parts of the tableau.

Probably the best known of these new sources are the Dead Sea Scrolls. The Scrolls were the library of a Jewish sectarian community which conducted a communal life in the stark Judean desert, near the Dead Sea. They form the largest group of ancient Jewish manuscripts we possess, and no other comparable manuscripts are known before the end of the first millennium C.E. They are firmly dated since it is known on archaeological grounds that the settlement at Khirbet Qumrân, where the Scrolls were discovered, was destroyed by the Romans in the year 68 C.E. They were all written, therefore, before that date, and the oldest of them were copied in the third century B.C.E. Thus, these manuscripts come from the period we are studying and the surprising light they cast on it will be examined below.

A second, relevant, manuscript discovery has also been made in recent decades. This collection of manuscripts dates from the period after 400 C.E., but many of the texts in them were composed considerably before that date. They are written in the Coptic language (the last stage of the development of ancient Egyptian, written in Greek letters) and were found at a place called Nag Hammadi in Egypt. This group of manuscripts contains some fifty-odd compositions of a Gnostic character. Most of these writings were originally composed in Greek and subsequently translated into Coptic.

Gnosticism was a widespread religious movement that took on multifarious forms from the second century C.E. on. Its roots are older and must, in part, go back to Jewish sources. In its Christian form, Gnosticism posed the major challenge to that form of Christian teaching which eventually came to be considered orthodox. There were also Jewish and pagan forms of Gnostic religion. Like the Essenes who wrote the Dead Sea Scrolls, the Gnostics were an esoteric community, keeping their teachings and books secret and revealing them only to the initiated. Until the Coptic Gnostic manuscripts from Nag Hammadi were discovered, virtually all that was known of the Gnostics was what could be inferred from the attacks on them by their opponents. The Coptic Gnostic manuscripts, then, provide first-hand insights into a religious movement which was known from outside sources alone. The similarity to the Dead Sea Scrolls and our knowledge of the Essenes is notable. The translations of all these documents have been published within recent months. Even preliminary studies indicate that their contribution to the understanding of Judaism is much more striking than could have been expected; their implications are only now starting to be worked out, but they promise exciting things for the future.

These two great manuscripts finds are by far the most important new sources which have become available to the historian of Judaism over recent decades. There have been other discoveries as well, including archaeological, epigraphical and similar direct material evidence. There are also contributions which have been made by the re-examination of known sources and texts in light of the newly discovered material. From a multiplicity of sources, and utilizing the contributions of varied fields of learning, a new picture of Judaism in the period of the Second Temple is emerging, and it is this new picture which will be sketched here.

2

THE AGE

The term "period of the Second Temple" refers, strictly speaking, to the age extending from the beginning of the Restoration, the return of the Jews from the Babylonian exile (536 B.C.E.), down to the destruction of the Temple in Jerusalem by the Romans under Titus in the year 70 C.E. Some scholars use the term differently to denote one or another part of this age, which they regard as having particular prominence, but here we shall adhere to its strict meaning. The examination of the religious and intellectual history of Judaism during this period is our chief aim, but it can only be pursued in its proper context. Consequently we must first sketch the general outline of the broad political and chronological canvas against which the history of Judaism must be painted. Necessarily this sketch must be only of the most prominent lines; it is not our intention here to write about kings and wars, about economics or power structures, but to examine some aspects of the history of ideas and religious culture.

The Jews were, in broadest terms, newcomers into the Fertile Crescent. The people of Israel are first mentioned on an Egyptian stele in trans-Jordan shortly before 1200 B.C.E. By that time there had been two thousand years of sophisticated written culture, of literature, science, medicine, and other sorts of intellectual creativity in the area, the great repositories of which were Egypt and Mesopotamia. The recent find of thousands of clay tablets at Ebla, dating from the third millennium B.C.E. highlights this. If one examines the fairly rough pottery of the Israelites during the period from the conquest to the destruction of the First Temple (Iron Age) and compares it with the highly wrought and delicate ware made by the inhabitants of Canaan during the preceding Late Bronze Age, one realises Israel's newness. The Jews set up a kingdom in the land of Canaan, and that kingdom soon split into two. The northern part, called Israel, was destroyed by the Assyrians in 722 B.C.E. The southern, called Judah, continued to exist as an independent political entity until conquered by the neo-Babylonian empire in the year 586 B.C.E.

Within half a century, Babylonian power itself was overthrown by a new force on the world scene, the Persians, who established an empire greater than any of their predecessors. Under the Persians the Jews, who had been exiled to Babylonia, were allowed to return to the land of Israel. This was now called the Persian district of Judah, and was part of the satrapy of the Cis-Euphrates. The return, which started in 536 B.C.E., continued with various ups and downs until the period about 400 B.C.E. The great leaders of Judaism at that time, the biblical record relates, were Ezra and Nehemiah, both appointees of the Persian court. Judah continued as a Persian province until the Persian empire fell to Alexander the Great in 332 B.C.E.

At this time, in the heartland of the old northern kingdom, there was another Persian district, Samaria, also inhabited by worshippers of the God of Israel. The Samaritans and the Judahites (later Judaeans, hence Jews) were in conflict, and the split between them became final some time between the fourth and second centuries B.C.E.

The Persian empire established by Cyrus (538–529 B.C.E.) and Darius I (522–486 B.C.E.) was the largest in history up to its time, in the Near East at least. The Persians took certain steps in the organization of it which were to be most important in the coming centuries. They established a bureaucracy which, through its checks and balances, managed to survive and function for two hundred years. Certain things were central to this system—including good communications. The communications were guaranteed by a network of royal roads which linked the different parts of the kingdom together, as well as by a system of royal couriers. One may recall how King Ahasuerus passed the word of his decree to the inhabitants of all the one hundred and twenty-seven provinces of his Empire (so the *Book of Esther* tells us). The letters were written in the name of King Ahasuerus and sent "by mounted couriers riding swift horses that were used in the king's service" (*Esther* 8:10). Moreover, these letters, like Mordechai's later missives, were read out to the subject populations, each in its own language (*ibid.* vs.9). One may presume that this was something like the way royal communications were actually transmitted.

It is worth remembering that the safety of travel and the security of trade are good criteria for judging the success of an ancient government (or, for that matter, a modern one). The Persians took steps to ensure both. The Persians also established a common language for the large area they administered—this was Aramaic. While the Mesopotamian empires had utilized various languages written in cuneiform script, it was the royal chancellery of the Persians which standardized the less cumbersome Aramaic language as the *lingua franca* of the east. Aramaic is a Semitic language written in the alphabetic script that had been developed in the preceding millennium, early forms of which served to write ancient Hebrew, Phoenician and other languages. The "chancellery" or official Aramaic handwriting style of the Persian bureaucracy became the basis for many later alphabets, including the square script used for Hebrew up to the present day and the Arabic script.

These steps taken by the Persians led to a greater amount of intercourse between the different parts of the empire than had been possible under previous rules. There was also a third element of Persian imperial policy that was to prove most

important, namely their policy of religious tolerance. As
distinct from the empires which preceded them, they did not
see their victory in war as the victory of their god over that of
the vanquished. So they seem to have changed the old policy
of eastern empires in which political domination also meant
religious repression. Two hundred years earlier, when Josiah,
king of Judah, cleaned the Assyrian gods out of the temple in
Jerusalem (621 B.C.E.), he made a bid for political independence as well as for religious reform. The Persians, to the
contrary, encouraged local cults. Their support for the rebuilding of the temple in Jerusalem is well known. A letter in
Aramaic, written in the year 419 B.C.E., to the Jewish garrison
at Elephantini in Upper Egypt (at that time Jews served as
mercenary soldiers in foreign armies) instructs them in the
king's name to observe the Passover. The same policy can be
discerned in Persian actions towards the cults of the other
subject peoples as well. Moreover, the Persians recognized
the religious authorities of Judah as the central holders of
power, and the religious law of the temple received government sanction. Some have seen this as a major force in the
development of Jewish law.

It used to be a standard theme of western historiography
that the battles of Marathon (490 B.C.E.) and Thermopylai
and the great sea battle of Salamis (480 B.C.E.) saved the
west from the encroachment of the (allegedly corrupt) orient
under Persian hegemony. Certainly, that century which
opened in Greece with these great battles was one of the most
remarkable flowerings of human intellectual and artistic
achievement. In many respects fifth century Athens is un-
parallelled. But the way of looking at history which saw those
battles as the salvation of the west from the degenerate orient
was one which ignored the character of the culture of the Near
East. What is more, it ignored the events of the half millennium
that followed. In the fifth century, indeed, the west was
Greece; the east was the area we now call the Near East. By
the time that Roman rule was consolidated in the east, in the
first century B.C.E., the west was the Latin-speaking world

of Italy, North Africa, Spain, Gaul and so on; the east was the
Greek-speaking world which extended from the Greek peninsula to the further borders of Mesopotamia. This division, or
better, this movement of the line of division, signals the great
changes that took place with the conquest of Alexander.

By the end of the fifth century B.C.E., the Greek city-states
were exhausted by internecine war. Alexander's father,
Philip of Macedon, almost a barbarian in the eyes of the
cultured Athenians (read Demosthenes' *Phillipics*!), united
the Greek world for the first time, but he did so by force. When
his son, Alexander the Great, crossed the Hellespont and
defeated Darius III Codomannus, the last of the Achaemenid
Kings of Persia, in battle at Issus in 333 B.C.E., he became
heir not only to the land of Persia itself, but to all the territories
which had been under the rule of the Persian King of Kings.
These territories included Judah and Samaria as well as
Mesopotamia and Egypt. Alexander held his immense empire
together, but when he died, rivalry for power led to fighting
among his generals which lasted for twenty years. By 301
B.C.E. Alexander's empire had been split into a number of
independent kingdoms. A certain Ptolemy Lagus (Ptolemy I)
gained control of Egypt and established the Ptolemaic dynasty
there. Ptolemy I also controlled the land of Palestine up to the
northern borders of ancient Canaan. His great rival was
Seleucus, who consolidated his rule in Mesopotamia, Iran and
Syria, as far south as the northern border of Palestine. During
the following century there was intermittent fighting between
the Ptolemies and the Seleucids, with Palestine as a chief
bone of contention. Eventually the Seleucids took control of
Palestine after the battle of Paneion (Banias) in 198 B.C.E.,
and held the land down to the outbreak of the Maccabean
revolt, a quarter of a century later.

Seleucid rule was at first well received by the Jews. For a
number of reasons, however, relations between the Seleucid
kings and their Jewish subjects degenerated. Motivated by a
desire to foster the Hellenization of Judea, the Seleucid king
Antiochus IV Epiphanes enacted a series of decrees forbidding

certain central Jewish religious practices (168 B.C.E.). This action led to the outbreak of a revolt in Judea, ably guided by five brothers belonging to the priestly Maccabean family. The Maccabeans were skilful both in war and diplomacy, and by 141 B.C.E. Simon, the last surviving brother, achieved political independence for Judea and was crowned king. The Maccabean brothers had taken advantage of the chaotic state of the Seleucid kingdom after the death of Antiochus IV Epiphanes, and had gained political advantages by playing the pretenders to the Syrian throne off against one another. Moreover, they had early had the political sagacity to ally themselves with Rome, whose encroachment in the east was already noticeable.

The Maccabean or Hasmonean dynasty held power in Judaea down to 63 B.C.E. In that year Pompey, taking advantage of civil war in the country, took Jerusalem for Rome and deposed the last Hasmonean king. In his place, the Romans established a pro-Roman dynasty, most probably of Idumean origin, the Herodians. The Herodians ruled Judea and the surrounding areas as vassal kings of Rome for three generations, those of Antipater (47–43), of Herod (37–4 B.C.E.), and of his sons, the last of whom was Archelaus (4 B.C.E.–6 C.E.). In Judea they were thoroughly hated by most of their subjects, with good cause, and eventually were removed from power by Rome. Judea then came under direct Roman rule, governed by a prefect (later a procurator) who was subject to the authority of the Roman governor of Syria. Branches of the Herodian family, however, ruled elsewhere in Palestine up to the end of the first century C.E.

The corrupt rule of the procurators combined with an increased intensity of messianic expectation among the Jews to produce chronic instability in Roman Palestine. This situation is chronicled in detail by Josephus in his *Jewish War*. Open revolt flared up in 66 C.E., and lasted four years, ending with the devastation of Judea and the destruction of Jerusalem and the temple in the year 70 C.E.

A second revolt broke out in 132 C.E. under Bar Kochba

or Bar Kosiba. It resulted in even greater devastation than had its predecessor, but Jewish settlement did not disappear even then. Indeed, at this time the Jews of Palestine produced the basic work of Jewish legal and hermeneutical learning.

After the Christianization of the Roman Empire (traditionally under way by the time of Constantine, 311–313 C.E.), the situation of the Jews in Palestine became progressively less tenable; the Jewish community became weaker, but did not disappear. Its centre moved to the Galilee in the north, and Jewish activity continued in the land of Israel down to the Moslem conquest in the seventh century, and subsequently down to the time of the Crusades. Jewish political independence however, ended in 70 C.E. and was not to be restored until 1948.

These then are the temporal and political parameters: the province of Judah, later the Hasmonaean (Maccabean) Kingdom of the Jews, between the Restoration and the destruction of the second temple. At first it was a district of the great Persian satrapy or governorship of Cis-Euphrates, then a Ptolemaic possession, a Seleucid possession, an independent Jewish state, a vassal kingdom of Rome, and then part of the Roman province of Syria. In this half-millennium, however, more changed than the names of rulers. There was a major cultural revolution, a change which was to leave the world very different from what it had been.

When Alexander conquered the Persian empire, he set forth on the policy of Hellenization of that empire, and he laid out a pattern that was followed by his successors for centuries— Greek cities were established throughout the empire, and all who would accept Greek language and education became part of that culture. The term "Greek" signalled not ethnic origin, but cultural belonging. A uniform culture with uniform institutions was established throughout this great empire. A man could move from one end of it to the other and, provided that he did not go out among the peasants, he could speak the same language, would find people with the same religious and cultural assumptions and, in general, would belong. As we have observed, the process of influence was not only one-directional. It is true that during the first two centuries of Greek rule the great ancient cultures of the east remained quiescent. The power of the Greek intellect seems to have overawed the orientals. But there was, in fact, a gradually accelerating process of interaction between the new Hellenistic Greek culture and the age-old cults, myths and ways of the east. Some of the most important thinkers and intellectuals of the early Hellenistic period (say, between 400 and 200 B.C.E.), and certainly thereafter, were not Greek by origin, but orientals of one sort or another (See above, Chapter 1). By the last century B.C.E. the cultures of the east were expressing themselves in Greek terms; they were Hellenized and became great influences in the Graeco-Roman world. It is against this changing and developing picture of cultural and religious syncretism and mutual influence that we must evaluate the Judaism of the age with which we are concerned.

The issues after Alexander are those of the meeting between two powerful cultures—Hellenism and Judaism—and the patterns and modes of interrelationship that developed between them. The Jewish reaction to Hellenism ran the whole gamut from enthusiastic assimilation to pietistic rejection. The measure of influence ran the whole scale from the most superficial contacts to systematic attempts to create a synthesis of the two. In broadest terms, this is perhaps the most crucial of the issues in the history of Judaism of that age.

3

EXILE, RESTORATION AND THE BIBLE

Jewish history of the ancient period is divided by destructions of the Temple and by exiles. The Babylonian exile (586 B.C.E.), like those of a later date brought about by the Romans (70 and 135 C.E.), was and remains a central marker. Still, it would be naïve to think that, because we decide to mark two periods of history at a given point, somehow there is no continuity between the before and the after. Human beings exist and human culture continues: the divisions are for the historian's convenience. Moreover, the divisions which are made (as they usually are) on the basis of major political events, are not necessarily those which would be made on cultural, religious or other grounds. Indeed, the way we divide history into periods is obviously determined by the way we view events and the relationship between them: the divisions themselves are always artificial. This may be seen clearly from the following example.

What was probably the most momentous cultural and political event of the last 500 years B.C.E. was recognised only peripherally as a dividing line by Jewish historiography, namely, the conquest of the east by Alexander the Great. This conquest established a political pattern which persisted, *mutatis mutandis*, until the fall of Constantinople to the Turks in the fifteenth century; it established a cultural reality which continues even to the present day. Yet, if we examine the way that Jewish history of the period of the Second Temple is usually written, the conquest of Palestine by Alexander the Great in 332 B.C.E. is not treated as a dividing line. The Maccabean revolt is so treated, and this is justifiable from the inner-Jewish point of view on the basis of the change of political régime. Moreover, it is in the context of the Maccabean revolt that historians usually treat the relationship between Judaism and Hellenism, even though the land of Israel had been under Hellenistic rule for 150 years before that revolt occurred.

Here a second consideration comes into play, namely, the character and scope of the sources which are at our disposal. In simple terms, these determine what we know and what we do not know. What sources exist for the history of Judaism in the years between the Restoration and the building of the Second Temple and its destruction by Titus? What is their nature? Unless these questions are asked and answered it is impossible to realise what it is that they tell us and what it is that they do not tell—what we know and what we do not know.

The Jewish people bears a continuing national and cultural tradition. Unlike most of the peoples of the ancient Near East, it has preserved alive its own language and cultural heritage since antiquity. A great deal is known about ancient Mesopotamia. This is not because the present-day inhabitants of Mesopotamia—the Iraqis—preserve Akkadian or Babylonian traditions, culture or language. Instead, it is the outcome of two fortunate circumstances. First, that the inhabitants of ancient Mesopotamia wrote on clay tablets which, if baked, are able to withstand the ravages of nature rather well. Second, that, fortunately, some inscriptions survived written in two languages, Mesopotamian and another which was known. It was the study of such bilingual inscriptions that enabled scholars to decipher the cuneiform script. In other words, what is known of ancient Mesopotamia is known through archaeological discoveries and scholarly diligence, to which good luck has made a certain contribution. The Jews, however, alone preserved their ancient literature and language as a living part of their culture. One other group claims to be the

heirs and true transmitters of the traditions of ancient Israel—
the Samaritans. Their claims should not be dismissed out of
hand, but their survival only as a tiny group means that we
may leave them for the moment.

What is the literature that the Jewish people preserved?
First and foremost, the Hebrew Bible. This comprises books
and writings that were composed for the most part before
400 B.C.E. Since the Jewish and Samaritan traditions split
at some time before the second century B.C.E., it can con-
fidently be asserted that the Pentateuch (common both to
Jews and Samaritans) was generally accepted by the worshippers of the God of Israel at an early date. Yet, the Samaritans know almost nothing of the remaining books of the Bible,
even those that were indubitably written before the Babylonian Exile (586 B.C.E.). The Samaritans, however, were
reputed to come from the nothern part of the country, the
ancient kingdom of Israel, while the people exiled by King
Nebuchadnezzar of Babylon in 586 B.C.E. were driven out of
the south, that is, from the kingdom of Judah, and particularly
from Jerusalem. Therefore, if the Samaritans are ignorant of
certain biblical books of pre-exilic date, this may be due to
the provenance of these books. After all, the books and traditions preserved by the exiles were from Judah, from the south.
Hence, it seems reasonable to conclude that the books of the
Bible that survived from the period of the First Temple were
those that were acceptable to the men who were exiled. The
exiles were, moreover, above all, the aristocracy and the
intelligentsia and the urban dwellers of the south, whose
capital was Jerusalem. It would seem to follow that the
material from the time of the First Temple that survived was
that which was acceptable to the bearers of the intellectual
tradition primarily in Jerusalem in the sixth century. Similarly,
later biblical books were presumably those acceptable to their
heirs.

It is important to note that the Hebrew Bible as we have it
does not represent the total literary or intellectual production
of the Jewish people in the period of the First Temple or of the

age of the Restoration (i.e. from earliest times down to about 400 B.C.E.). Within Scripture itself mention is made of other books and writings, for example, the "Book of the Wars of the Lord" or "The Royal Chronicles". Alas, none of them has survived. This absence of any surviving sources other than the Bible is noteworthy. And, furthermore, it is not relieved for the period of the First Temple by any epigraphic discoveries. There are very few inscriptions stemming from that age which are of any substantial importance for the writing of religious or intellectual history. And this is also true for the age of the Restoration. Indeed, the dearth of written materials from the land of Israel in this entire period is quite remarkable. It is, no doubt, due partly to the use of perishable, organic materials as media for writing. Moreover, it may be a matter of chance that no find has been made; and a lucky archaeological discovery may reverse the situation.

However this may be, it is true that for the whole of Jewish history down to the end of the fifth or the early fourth century B.C.E., the only major literary source of information is the canonical tradition of the Hebrew Bible. It is clear to anyone who reads the writings of the Prophets that there were other types of religious activity going on throughout this period than those which were approved by the authors and the transmitters of the biblical tradition—the views of the latter being represented by the Prophets. But, in fact, nothing is known of these other views beyond what can be gleaned from the Prophets' polemic against them. There are, we repeat, no sources of information beyond those which were acceptable to certain groups in Jerusalem in the period before the Babylonian exile and that which followed it. The selectivity of these sources is also evident in other respects. They reflect nothing certain concerning the views of "the man in the street"—no public opinions polls determined his views. Indeed, the actual religious belief and practice of the average city or country dweller might have differed quite considerably from those of the intellectual or learned groups responsible for the production or preservation of biblical literature.

In the next chapter we shall deal with some questions which arise when scholars set out to describe Judaism in the period from about 200 B.C.E., for which age the sources surviving increase dramatically in volume and variety. For that period, paradoxically, the difficulties seem to be the reverse of those encountered by the historian of the period down to 400 B.C.E. Until very recent times, the years between 400 B.C.E. and 200 B.C.E. were a sort of "Dark Ages". The surviving sources were sparse and gave little insight into religious, intellectual or social history. This situation has been somewhat relieved in the last few years by the publication of certain of the Dead Sea Scrolls and the reassessments these have brought about. Nevertheless, those two centuries remain somewhat obscure.

It has been questionable whether the emphasis placed by many biblical scholars in past generations on the contrast between the religion of Israel before and after the Babylonian exile was justified. These scholars maintained that Judaism changed from the religion of the Prophets—the exalted ethical monotheism of Second Isaiah—to a religion of law. According to this view, legalistic religion was already developing in the writings of the prophet Ezekiel, who devotes so much of his book to the sanctuary and sacrificial and cultic regulations. This developing legalism was typified by the priestly source in the Pentateuch, and was formalized for future generations by the promulgation of the law under Ezra. Other students of the period would locate the beginning of the development of the Oral Law, of the institution of the synagogue, of the self-consciousness of Israel as the separate "holy seed" in this age.

Enough has been written (although perhaps the lesson is still not thoroughly learned) about the motives which made a balanced understanding of the function of law in Judaism unusual among Christian scholars, and an understanding of the role of the Temple and its ritual rare, particularly in those Protestant circles which have been so influential in the development of modern scholarly study of the Bible. The priestly source of the Pentateuch is today widely recognized to contain very old elements indeed; modern understandings of the growth of legal systems and comparative studies in the development of code law systems teach us that a process of interpretation of law must have been coeval with its promulgation and application. Indeed, frequently the codification or promulgation of a set of laws followed upon a long process of priestly or other interpretation, often esoteric in character.

It is not denied here that after the Babylonian exile Judaism changed. Nonetheless, the continuities between the community of the Restoration and that of pre-exilic Judah have not been adequately stressed. After all, people who were exiled at the time of Nebuchadnezzar in 586 B.C.E. could have returned at the time of the edict of Cyrus in 536 B.C.E. Psalmodic composition continued throughout this age; prophecy went on until after 400 B.C.E. Historiographic rehearsal of the past of Israel for present theological purposes was still carried on, as may be seen in the Books of Chronicles and Ezra-Nehemiah. Continuities in religious institutions and types of religious creativity between these two periods were marked, in spite of the real and obvious differences between the political and social realities.

One might venture to speculate that, after the Restoration, the change from the socio-religious institutions of an earlier age was a gradual one as the new situation made its impact. The consciousness of this gradual change in institutions may have brought about the process of collection and editing of sacred traditions, particularly the gathering of the prophetic writings and the assembling and editing of the wisdom tradition and other parts of the *Ketubim* or "Writings", the third of the parts of which the Hebrew Bible is composed. Sacred traditions were becoming books, even sacred books, and a basic change in the nature of Judaism took place once the idea of the sacred book became securely established. This did not happen suddenly, however, and perhaps not the exile itself so much as the changed social and political conditions of the community of the Restoration brought about this gradual process of change and adaptation within Judaism.

The historical sources preserved in the Bible peter out after 400 B.C.E., and the next period about which we have detailed knowledge starts around 200 B.C.E. By that time almost all biblical writing was concluded and new, radically different, forms of religious writing emerged, of which the apocalypse, the *pesher* commentary, and others are examples. Changes in the social and religious structure were far-reaching; groups like the Pharisees, Saducees and Essenes appeared during the second century; innovations which were to set the patterns for the succeeding millennia were to be found. In the field of religious ideas alone, dualism, determinism, apocalyptic eschatology in full form, problems of the nature of providence and the purposiveness of creation were to the fore. One reason why the difference between the fifth and second centuries seemed so acute was the hiatus in the sources, the "Dark Ages" which were the fourth and third centuries B.C.E. Nonetheless, even when this is taken into account, the contrast between the age down to 400 B.C.E. and the picture to be observed after 200 B.C.E. is stark, indeed even starker than that between Judaism before and after the Babylonian exile.

4

NEW LIGHT ON THE THIRD CENTURY

The situation created by the character of the sources results in a lacuna in our knowledge not only of the religious and intellectual history of Judah in the fourth and third centuries B.C.E., but also of its social, political and economic history. These latter areas of knowledge have been somewhat illuminated by two finds of papyri. One lot, in Greek, comes from Egypt and contains the reports sent by Zenon, the steward of Apollonius, the "finance minister" of Ptolemy II Philadelphus, about his dealings with Palestine and the trips he made to that country on his master's behalf, including an extensive journey in the year 259 B.C.E. This body of texts sheds some light on economic and social matters, but is of little or no help to the historian of ideas or religion.

The second group of texts is the so-called Dāliyeh papyri, named after the area of the Jordan rift where they were found, some miles north of Jericho. These were copied in the fourth century B.C.E., and are predominantly legal documents written in the Aramaic language. They were taken by refugees who fled from Samaria before Alexander in the year 331 B.C.E., and whose bones, together with the papyri, were found in a cave. They have not yet been published in full, but according to the preliminary reports they seem unlikely to contribute much to our knowledge of matters other than chronological or legal affairs. In these latter realms, however, their importance is considerable. What is evident already, from the Wadi Dāliyeh texts and even more from the Zenon papyri, is that the process of Hellenization was well under way at the end of the fourth and early in the third centuries B.C.E., and started to some extent, even before Alexander the Great. It is difficult to learn more than this, however, about matters of religious or intellectual interest.

In addition to these two papyrus discoveries, in recent years there have been a number of attempts by scholars to penetrate into the social and religious history of the fourth and third centuries. One such attempt works back from the first period at which the historical sources become relatively abundant again, after 200 B.C.E. When the situation in Maccabean Judea is examined, what first strikes even the most super- ficial student is the bitter conflict between Judaism and Hell- enism that characterized the early part of the second century B.C.E. This conflict became so intense as to lead to open warfare in the Maccabean revolt.

The Maccabean revolt, these historians point out, cannot have been the result of a sudden development. Their view is that the conflict was basically one between Hellenizing and anti-Hellenizing parties in Jerusalem itself, although other factors (notably Seleucid policy) may have played a role. There is a good deal to be said for this view. The forces that eventually exploded in revolt in 175 B.C.E. must have been building up tension in Jewish society for a considerable period of time. The process of the Hellenization discerned in the Dāliyeh, and particularly in the Zenon papyri, must have been fostered by groups or circles in Judean society, just as groups which opposed Hellenism must have arisen in reaction to it. Thus, the pietistic trends and groups represented at the start of the Maccabean revolt by the Hasideans must have had a "pre-history".

At the start of the Maccabean uprising, these groups observed the Sabbath with such rigour that they allowed themselves to be killed rather than desecrate it by taking up arms to oppose their enemies. Groups which developed the sort of approach that made this action seem necessary cannot have arisen spontaneously. Some scholars have maintained that they must have originated in the third century B.C.E. This is an important insight which contributes notably to our understanding of the social and religious situation in the third century B.C.E. Unfortunately, some of those espousing this view have made it into the general principle by which they analyse and describe all aspects of the period preceding the Maccabean revolt. At the point at which this happens doubts begin to arise.

One matter that has been intimately tied to the Maccabean revolt and particularly to the Hasideans is the origin of apocalyptic literature. This is a type of writing which was widespread in Jewish circles in the last pre-Christian centuries. It had considerable vogue, furthermore, in Jewish and Christian circles alike through most of the first millennium C.E. The remarks made here will bear on the oldest part of this continuous literary tradition. The apocalypses are typically presented as a literature of visions written in the name of an ancient sage, that is to say that they are pseudepigraphic in form. These books revealed the secrets of the heavens and the earth, including information about the end of days. Studies continue in the attempt to reach a clear formulation of the characteristics of the literary *genre* of the apocalypse. Among its most typical features are a mysteriousness of form, eso-tericism (often assumed) and symbolic visions, most often interpreted by an angelic mediator, and sometimes very complicated indeed. Moreover, the authors of this literature frequently wrote under the deep impression that the end of days was imminent. This attitude is not found in all the apocalypses, but is prevalent in many of them. The apocalypses were a major vehicle of theological and conceptual innovation in the Second Temple period.

The view that asserts the dominance of conflict concerning Hellenism in third century Judaism and the antiquity of the Hasidean type of pietism, also attributes the first group of apocalypses to these pietists. Generally the apocalypses are regarded as a new phenomenon, emerging from the crisis engendered by the persecutions by Antiochus IV Epiphanes, King of Syria, and the revolt that followed. These persecutions and the martyrdoms which came in their train produced an intolerable situation: the righteous were suffering and dying for their very righteousness. Out of this the apocalypses were born; it is the eschatological message of vindication that lies at the heart of the apocalypses.

We have noted above that almost all the sources from which Judaism of the period of the First Temple and the age of the Restoration is known are biblical (Chapter 3). Moreover, when the Judaism of the period after 200 B.C.E. is compared with that of the age of the Restoration before 400 B.C.E., it exhibits very striking innovations, not the least among which is the apocalyptic literature. Now, in contrast with the sources for the earlier period, which are all biblical, the sources for the "surprising" Judaism after 200 B.C.E. are all preserved outside the Hebrew Bible. (Regarding Daniel and its evidence, see below Chapter 5.) With scarcely an exception, they are not cherished by the Jewish tradition, but have been transmitted by the various Christian churches. Some have come to light through archaeological chance. This means, of course, that when the extra-biblical literature of the period after 200 B.C.E. shows us dimensions of religious thought which are new in comparison with that of an earlier age, various explanations may be sought. They could be new developments in Judaism, either indigenous or under the influence of foreign cultures—Greek, Persian or even Phoenician. They could well also be the first literary expression of points of view and attitudes which may have existed from earlier days, but which are not reflected by the biblical sources, due to the selectivity with which these latter were transmitted.

Against this series of problems, the recent publication of the manuscripts of the *Book of Enoch*, from among the Dead Sea Scrolls, must be assessed. The original Semitic text of this writing was lost in antiquity, along with all but fragments of the Greek translation of it. Some quotations of the Greek have survived. The first is in the New Testament (Jude vs.14), while the most extensive are passages quoted by the Byzantine chronographers, particularly the ninth century writer, George the Syncellus. We do not know why the Greek text disappeared, but George the Syncellus does not seem to have had direct access to it. Instead, like many Byzantine authors, he drew his quotations from those incorporated in the writings of the chronographers who preceded him, in a tradition going back to Eusebius. Two papyri of the middle of the first millennium C.E. also contain some parts of this Greek text.

The text of the *Book of Enoch* first became widely and completely known with the recovery, publication and translation of its Ethiopic text in the late eighteenth and early nineteenth centuries by the English scholar, Richard Laurence. The book is replete with material for the understanding of Judaism. Among the Dead Sea Scrolls, fragments of ten or so manuscripts of the *Book of Enoch* were discovered and were recently published by their appointed editor, J. T. Milik. Much of interest is to be learned from these manuscripts. Of immediate significance here are their dates. The *Book of Enoch*, as it is preserved in Ethiopic, is a compendium of five separate writings. The first and third parts of it survive at Qumrân in manuscripts clearly dated in the late third or early second century B.C.E. on palaeographic grounds. They are not the authors' original autographs, but copies of them or copies of copies of them. Consequently, these two parts of the *Book of Enoch* must have been composed by the third century at the latest. Moreover, the first part of the *Book of Enoch*, the so-called *Book of the Watchers* (i.e. the fallen angels, Genesis 6:1–2) is a composite literary work whose author has taken advantage of sources he had before him. This can readily be discerned in the text of the book. It follows, of course, that these sources which are already combined in our oldest manuscript must be even earlier.

From this it also follows that these parts of the *Book of Enoch* are the oldest surviving Jewish documents of religious character outside the Bible. They are the chief evidence we now possess for Judaism in the third century B.C.E., and they were written well before the Maccabean revolt. Their importance is manifold, and some aspects of it will be explored.

What do these documents, then, contain? The *Book of the Watchers* contains various sorts of information. At its heart is the story of the fallen angels, the "sons of God" of Genesis 6:1–2, who sinned with the daughters of men; the secret information which they revealed to women; and the corruption which their bastard offspring of giants brought about. This story had wide circulation in connection with Enoch and Noah, and it recurs elsewhere in the literature associated with Enoch. It is also found in the *Book of Jubilees* (an early second century B.C.E. composition) and other later sources. This body of legend served various purposes. One was etiological— it dealt with the origins of evil, of various forbidden teachings, of demons (the spirits of the giants who drowned in the Flood), of illness (*Jubilees* 10:1–15), and more. It most probably also preserved ancient mythological traditions of a "Prometheus" or culture-hero type, and also of a heavenly revolt.

The *Book of the Watchers* reports the ascent of Enoch to the heavenly realm and his experiences there. He reaches the presence of God and witnesses the steps taken by Him against the Watchers and their offspring. This section of the book is important since it is the oldest Jewish ascent vision. The Hebrew Bible records various types of religious experience such as visions, dreams, bodily transportations, auditions and others. It does not contain any visions relating in detail the ascent of the recipient of the vision to the heavens, a type of experience which was widespread in a number of surrounding cultures. This absence of the ascent vision has been attributed to the fact that the view of man in the Hebrew Bible does not distinguish between body and soul in such a way as to set them in opposition or contrast, or even to regard the soul as the essential part of man. As noted above, this distinction was known to the Greeks from the sixth or fifth centuries B.C.E. on, and was particularly current in the Hellenistic age. Admittedly, we have ascent visions recorded (in later texts) in which it is not clear whether the ascent was in the body or not in the body (compare Paul's words in 2 Cor 12:2–3) Nonetheless, it seems notable that this type of religious experience should start to appear in Jewish texts in an age when the idea of the separable soul had considerable currency. Thus, the ascent vision of Enoch represents the first occurrence of a type of religious experience which became very prevalent in later times. It also seems to mark a change in the view of man which was to have very considerable repercussions.

In this vision there is a description of the divine palace, the heavenly environs of God, through which the visionary ascends. The experience peaks in the vision of the Throne of God and in the revelation which Enoch receives there. The oldest Jewish mystical texts are called the *Merkabah* or "Chariot" texts. The term "Chariot" was the name given to the winged throne of God, described by the prophet Ezekiel (Ezek 1). Indeed, as was pointed out some decades ago, the "Chariot" texts employ a very distinctive technical terminology to describe the environs of God. This terminology derives from the first chapter of the Book of Ezekiel, and the speculation based on that chapter was a constitutive element of this oldest type of Jewish mystical writing.

The "Chariot" mystical books have been dated to the middle of the first millennium C.E., the later Talmudic period. G. G. Scholem demonstrated that this terminological tradition could be traced back into early rabbinic sources, and into still earlier works dated in the late pre-Christian period. Fragments of a writing entitled the *Angelic Liturgy* from among the Dead Sea Scrolls showed that this same terminological tradition was known in the circles which produced the Scrolls. It is also found to exist in a developed form in Chapter 14 of the *Book of Enoch*, part of the *Book of the Watchers*. This means that it was not just the idea of a heavenly ascent which was well developed by the time that this part of the *Book of Enoch* was written, in the third century B.C.E. at the latest. It also demonstrates the antiquity of the tradition of speculation upon the Chariot vision of Ezekiel as the mode by which the heavenly realm is to be described and which was already well formulated by the third century B.C.E., many years before anyone thought that it could have happened.

It is quite important to be clear that this does not mean that mysticism was practised in Jewish circles in the third century B.C.E. The ascent vision and the terminology for the description of the heavenly realm are shared by the *Book of Enoch*, Chapter 14, and by the "Chariot" mystical texts. The end or purpose of the ascent differs. One great authority has described the purpose of ascent in the "Chariot" books as the "perception of (God's) appearance on the Throne, as described by Ezekiel, and the cognition of the mysteries of the celestial throne world" (Scholem, *Major Trends*, p.44). In Enoch's case, however, the purpose of the ascent is the revelation of certain matters having to do first and foremost with the Watchers and their fate.

The biblical writings do not exhibit any interest in the technical description of the environs of the Godhead as seen by a visionary. This sort of interest was already well developed, however, by the third century, a fact which casts a rather unexpected light into the gloom of those dark centuries. The Bible does show some interest, however, in the associated matter of angelology, and peripherally in demonology. In the *Book of Enoch* these spirit realms are well represented. The archangels are known by name, and are very active, while the origins and functions of demons are much discussed.

Following the vision of the divine Throne and the punishment of the Watchers, Enoch is taken on two "guided tours". First, he sees visions of the underworld, the secrets of meteorology, the place of the fallen angels and their punishment and, finally, the names of the archangels and their tasks (Chapters 17–20). On his second journey, he sees again the places where the angels are punished, Sheol and sundry distant places, parts of the mythological geography of earth, with special emphasis on their meteorological and astronomical features (Chapters 26–36). From this material, the range of interests of the *Book of the Watchers* is evident. There is also some eschatological interest, particularly in Chapters 1–6 and 10:14–16;

this latter section, however, is not truly eschatological, for it describes events which will take place before the flood. Furthermore, these chapters contain the oldest known fragments of Jewish biblical exegesis. But it is the range of scientific (or, better, "pseudo-scientific") material in them that is astounding, and the impression made by it is reinforced by the contents of the other Enochic writing which stems from the third century, the *Astronomical Book*. In this writing, which was about twice as long in its Aramaic form (unfortunately mostly lost) as in its Ethiopic version, the sort of "learned" information referred to above abounds. It is full of astronomy and meteorology and calendary lore. The whole of the *Astronomical Book* is in the form of a heavenly journey upon which Enoch embarks under the tutelage of the archangel Uriel.

From these two writings, it is clear that there existed in the third century B.C.E. broad areas of speculation of a pseudo-scientific kind in Judah and in Jewish circles. That they originate in Judah, in Jewish circles, is the most likely view; a Samaritan origin seems unlikely. Considered thus, these documents are quite surprising. The picture of a rather sophisticated and rich realm of speculation and "sacred science" within Judaism, the highly developed ascent vision and the broad interest in "scientific" matters are totally unexpected. Moreover, the documents in which these interests are presented are apocalypses. The new publications of the manuscripts of the *Book of Enoch*, then, force us to a re-assessment of the complexion of third century Judaism and of the origins of apocalyptic literature. The origins of apocalyptic literature have been to the fore of scholarly debate in recent years. These parts of the *Book of Enoch* are the oldest surviving apocalypses. They ante-date the apocalyptic parts of the Book of Daniel by half a century at least, and their evidence must be brought into account in any assessment of the development of apocalyptic literature.

5

ENOCH AND APOCALYPTIC ORIGINS

In the last chapter we looked at the nature and character of Judaism in the third century B.C.E. as illuminated by the recently published manuscripts from among the Dead Sea Scrolls. The range of interests thus uncovered will probably be broadened and deepened as further manuscripts from Qumrân are published. It seems very likely that the Aramaic *Testament of Levi* also stems from the third century, and perhaps other works will be added to this corpus as scholarship advances. The *Testament of Levi*, purporting to be the last will and testament of Jacob's son, is known in Aramaic from fragmentary manuscripts found in the famous Cairo Geniza. The Geniza was a repository for old books, papers and letters which was found in a synagogue in Cairo at the end of the last century. It contained an incomparable collection of thousands of fragments of Jewish writings from the Middle Ages.

A number of manuscripts from the Geniza have been identified as containing writings from a sectarian library like that of Qumrân. It seems most likely that a mediaeval discovery of some Dead Sea Scrolls was made and that copies of writings from this find eventually made their way into the Geniza. These include the *Damascus Document* (a clearly sectarian work) and most probably the Hebrew fragments of Ben Sira (Ecclesiasticus) and the Aramaic *Testament of Levi*. A Greek translation of some parts of this last writing is known, and a number of fragmentary Aramaic manuscripts of it have turned up at Qumrân. It, or a closely affiliated writing, must have been one of the sources of the *Book of Jubilees*, and also of the Greek *Testament of Levi* (a different work), which is included in the Greek writing called the *Testaments of the Twelve Patriarchs*.

The Aramaic *Testament of Levi*, then, only exists in fragments. It is instructive for the character of very ancient Jewish biblical exegesis. It also contains long and detailed instructions, supposedly given by Abraham to Isaac and transmitted to Levi. These instructions deal with a sacrificial cult which these patriarchs supposedly conducted. In a great many of their details these instructions differ from everything else known of Jewish sacrificial law. They also show some otherwise unknown material of botanical character, here related to the types of wood which are to be used for the fire upon the altar. This document also presents some Messianic expectations, all concentrated on a descendant of Levi who is expected at the end. It is written, like the manuscripts of the Book of Enoch, in the literary Aramaic of the age and, incidentally, contains what is probably the most ancient Aramaic poetry known.

The Aramaic *Testament of Levi* is not as firmly dated to the third century B.C.E., however, as are the manuscripts of the *Book of Enoch*. These are clearly third century, a dating established first and foremost by the palaeographic dating of their script; it may be that once the Aramaic *Testament of Levi* manuscripts are published in full, we will be able to date it with greater precision. But, even basing observations only on the manuscripts of the *Book of Enoch*, one must raise certain issues relating to the character of Judaism in earlier ages. For these, only the biblical sources survive, and their purpose or intent is certainly not to give a sampling of all types of Jewish culture and learning, but rather to promote or preserve certain very specific types of tradition and teaching. An example of a case where it may be possible to penetrate beyond the biblical text is in the Bible's representation of the figure of Enoch.

Enoch is first introduced by a few verses in the Book of Genesis (Gen.5:21–24). He then reappears in a series of sources, mostly written from the second century B.C.E. onwards. It had been an open question whether the figure of Enoch as found in the sources from the early second century on was to be seen as a development of that age. Some scholars, pointing to the fact that Enoch is seventh from Adam, and that in Mesopotamian tradition the seventh antediluvian king was a wisdom figure, sought the origins of the traditions about Enoch in Mesopotamia. Indeed, there is an accumulation of new and older evidence which makes it appear quite probable that the scientific and learned traditions, with which we know that Enoch was associated at least from the third century, have strong Mesopotamian connections.

Two independent studies of the Mesopotamian sources suggest that an extensive tradition of learning was attached to Enoch because he was patterned after certain mythological Mesopotamian wisdom figures. Other scholars have commented that the scientific theories of the *Astronomical Book* were of Mesopotamian character and show no influence of the much more advanced Greek science of the Hellenistic age. These observations, incidentally, were based solely on the Ethiopic text of the *Astronomical Book*. Now that the more ancient, longer Aramaic form of the book is partly available, a renewed examination of this matter seems called for. The *Book of the Watchers* assumes a particular mythological map of the world, over which Enoch travels, particularly in the second of his two journeys. This map of the world is most closely related to Mesopotamian geographic conceptions. At a different level of discussion, the *Book of the Giants*, another of the Enochic writings from Qumrân, mentions Mesopotamian mythological personalities, including Gilgamesh.

All of this indicates that the learned tradition nurtured in certain Jewish circles by the third century B.C.E., if not rather earlier, was largely Mesopotamian in character, although expressed in our sources in Aramaic. It was associated with

Enoch, who was already mentioned in the Bible, yet it seems abundantly clear that the figure of Enoch as he appears in the later sources is not just an exegetical development of Genesis 5:21–24. The growth of the figure of Enoch must be tied to the learned tradition of the age. It remains an open question whether this presentation of Enoch was itself a development of that tradition about him hinted at by the author of Genesis 5, some centuries earlier, rather than of Genesis itself. If due weight is given to the Mesopotamian evidence, this is not unlikely.

Another interesting parallel to the development of the Enoch figure is that of Daniel. The Book of Daniel is composed of two parts. The stories (Chapters 1–6) were written by the third century at the latest, while the visions (Chapters 7–12) come from the time of the Maccabean revolt (after 168 B.C.E.). Daniel is the purported author of the book, which is set in the time of the Babylonian and Persian monarchies. Yet the selection of this particular pseudepigraphic author is strange, for the Daniel figure of the Book of Daniel has no obvious antecedent in other biblical literature. The identity of the Moses of a Moses pseudepigraphon, or of an Elijah, or an Ezra, in the books attached to them, was clear, but who was Daniel?

Among the Dead Sea Scrolls tiny fragments of one work (and perhaps more) attributed to Daniel have turned up. They seem to be similar in character to the biblical book, but not identical with it. Again, the Greek translations of Daniel contain some stories not to be found in the form of the book which is preserved in the Hebrew Bible. These compositions were not necessarily (and not even probably) written under the inspiration of the canonical Book of Daniel. Instead, they show that the Book of Daniel was part of a wider literature whose hero or pseudepigraphic author was Daniel. So the question of his identity becomes even more intriguing. There was a mythological Canaanite wise man called Dan'il, mentioned in second millennium Ugaritic epics and by the Book of Ezekiel, but his relationship to the Daniel of the biblical and apocryphal sources is tenuous. The *Book of Jubilees*, interestingly enough, knows Dan'il as Enoch's father-in-law.

Here, then, are two figures, Enoch and Daniel, who may have roots going back into mythological antiquity, and both of whom seem to reach special development in the late Persian or early Hellenistic periods. Both have wisdom dimensions, both reveal divine secrets and witness to the truth of the God of Israel. The parallel between them is quite striking. These developments of the pre-Maccabean age must come into account in re-exploring "dark ages" of post-exilic Judaism.

As a conclusion to this part of the discussion, it may be noticed that the development of a learned literature associated with a figure out of the ancient or mythological past is not limited to the Jewish sphere during the Hellenistic period. The Egyptian god of wisdom, Thoth, was identified with the Greek god Hermes, and a large literature of secret and revealed teaching was attributed to him. Similar, it appears, was the Phoenician god Taautos (see Eusebius, praep. ev. 1.9) who derived from Egyptian Thoth.

The publication of the new fragments of the *Book of Enoch*, then, serves to illustrate dramatically how dependent we are on the sources which have survived for our historical reconstructions, and how the character of these sources affects our reconstructions. The origins of the apocalyptic literature are not merely thrown back half a century or more as a result of these new data; the very character and context of its development must now be reassessed. Scholarly work in recent years has concentrated on the questions of the origins of apocalyptic eschatology, and on tracing its development from the future hope of the prophets. This particular issue has been at the centre of scholarly interest because of its importance for the study of Christianity and particularly of the New Testament, not for the study of the apocalypses.

The change from older forms of future hope into apocalyptic eschatology has been seen to result from the conflict between the groups in society which bore and nurtured the future hope of the prophets, and their environment. The new manuscripts of the *Book of Enoch* do not contradict this view; they are, however, the oldest existing Jewish apocalypses and the weight of their central interests lies elsewhere, not in the eschatological at all.

Some years ago, study of certain texts led me to maintain that the speculative interests are one of the core elements of the apocalypses. By the term "speculative interests" are intended such matters as cosmology, astronomy, calendar and so forth. Some scholars have suggested that a particular connection exists between the apocalyptic literature and that type of biblical and apocryphal literature called "wisdom literature". The wisdom literature comprises such books as Proverbs and Ecclesiastes, Ben Sira and the Wisdom of Solomon. In spite of the suggestive character of the term "wisdom literature", however, if in fact the preserved wisdom books are representative of the interests and concerns of the circles that produced them, then they were not particularly interested in these speculative matters. Now, the antiquity of the first and third parts of the *Book of Enoch* means that by the third century B.C.E. at the latest this speculative learning existed in Jewish circles; yet it seems amply clear that such interests as these were beyond the pale for the transmitters of biblical literature. The Book of Daniel, unique among the apocalypses for its lack of interest in such matters, is ample evidence of this; it is the only apocalypse that was accepted into the Bible. From this it seems to follow that to trace the eschatological axis as the chief one along which apocalyptic literature developed is to lay upon the evidence the same censorial rules as did the biblical editors themselves.

Instead, from consideration of the simple fact of the palaeographic dating of the Qumrân manuscripts of the *Book of Enoch* to the late third and early second centuries B.C.E., it can be inferred that this realm of speculative interest was much cultivated in pre-Maccabean Judea. Moreover, such speculations had reached a level of development such as to be embodied in the complex written form of the two oldest parts of the *Book of Enoch*. Furthermore, in the century after

Alexander, this type of knowledge was still permeated by the learned tradition of Mesopotamia as its astronomical and geographical views indicate. Suddenly, a quite unexpected dimension of the intellectual world of Judaism in the third (and perhaps the fourth) centuries B.C.E. is unveiled. How does this fit into the pictures that have been drawn in recent years of the social and religious organization of the Jewish people at that time? How does it affect our understanding of the development of Judaism and Jewish religious literature?

None of the recent attempts to reconstruct a picture of third century Judaism has taken this element into account. Generally, these attempts have tried to discern polemical tones in the literary remains or else have focussed on conflicts which were known to exist from the surviving historical sources. Attempts to write social and political history have been made by assuming that polemics or conflicts imply the existence of groups that carried them on. The conflicts that have been isolated as the basis for projecting the existence of such differing groups within the Jewish people have focussed on two issues—the nature of eschatological hope and assimilation or syncretism. The latter interest is clearly determined and, to a large extent justifiably, by the events of the early second century which climaxed in the Maccabean revolt (see above, Chapter 4). The former, like the attempt to describe apocalyptic literature in terms of eschatology alone, is determined in part by the interests of the authors of the biblical books and those who transmitted them. These gave the biblical text its particular emphases and content. Since the Bible very often plays a central role in the thinking of scholars of Judaism and early Christianity, the complexion laid upon it by those who transmitted it led to the interest in certain matters and lack of interest in others. The speculative and pseudoscientific matters are not present in the Bible. They are new in the post-biblical sources. They are almost completely absent from the New Testament. For these reasons in the history of scholarship scarcely any serious attempt has been made to understand this material and to study its role in the Judaism of its day.

It is quite evident, then, that groupings like pietistic and
Hellenizing Jews could scarcely have exhausted the types of
groups and trends in third century Judaism. The conservative
piety of a Ben Sira must have had a place in it, just as did the
speculations embodied in the *Book of Enoch.* The circles which
cultivated the latter must have been well learned; they may
also have had connections with the traditional intellectual
groups—the wise and the priests. Enoch is patterned, after all,
in the type of a wise man; indeed, he is the founder of wisdom.
A priestly connection may be suggested by the interest in
calendar, and astronomy. In the later Dead Sea sect, for
example, the interest in these matters was related to the
calculation of the sacred calendar and the service of the
priestly courses in the Temple. Such observations as these,
however, remain purely speculative; there is no firm evidence
for identifying the groups and circles which nurtured these
speculations.

As mentioned, their character as visions is central to the
apocalypses. This feature, more than any other, appeared to
speak for the origins of apocalyptic literature lying within the
prophetic tradition. Certainly by the time of Zechariah, if not
substantially by that of Ezekiel, most of the elements distinctive of the literary form of the apocalypse are to be found in
prophetic writing. In many ways the travels of Enoch described in the *Book of the Watchers* are close to Ezekiel, Chapters
40–48—this prophet's view of the ideal Jerusalem. This brings
to mind another priestly connection—speculation about
heavenly things is ancient when these things are related to the
idea of the heavenly pattern of the Temple and its furnishings.
This is clearly indicated already in Exodus and 2 Chronicles
and the idea that the earthly Temple is patterned after the
heavenly one has ancient, mythological roots. Now, however,
in light of the new manuscripts and their date, the view that
either the form or content of the apocalypses originated exclusively or predominantly from prophecy may well be strained.

In general, there seems no reason to think that the collection
of literature transmitted in the Hebrew Bible represents all

the types of Jewish literary creativity down to the third century B.C.E. Instead, it is a selection of texts, and that selection primarily reflects the judgement of certain groups in Jerusalem before and after the Babylonian exile. It seems specious, therefore, to seek the full explanation of a third or second century phenomenon from roots to be discerned in the Bible and, if such cannot be located, immediately to attribute it to foreign influence. Other circles than those responsible for the winnowing of biblical literature must have existed; the oldest extrabiblical books teach us that some of these were deeply involved in ascent vision activity and speculative sacred sciences. Such speculations had already taken on a sophisticated written form by the third century at the latest.

It had been observed in the past that those sections of the Bible which have closest relationship in form to the apocalypses show little contact with them in their eschatological type of content (e.g. Ezek 40–48; Zach 1–4; Ezek 16, 17, 19): on the other hand, those texts in which the development of apocalyptic eschatology can be traced seem to lack the formal elements of the apocalypses (e.g. Isaiah 24–37; Ezek 38–39; Isaiah 40–65; Zach 9–14). Could it be that formal elements of the apocalypses, which occur in full development in the *Book of the Watchers* and the *Astronomical Book*, were endowed with a heightened or almost exclusively eschatological content in response to the crisis brought about by the Antiochean persecution? The older parts of the *Book of Enoch* show some eschatological interest, but also exhibit a broad range of other concerns. It is the eschatological content that comes to play a central role in such writings as Daniel, the *Testament of Moses* and the *Dream Visions of Enoch*, which arose on exactly this background. We know of profound changes in eschatological views which came about at the same time.

The origins of the speculative material which plays such a large part in the oldest apocalypses is itself the subject of some speculation. It is certainly complex. A number of lines of development led into it, but at present it is difficult to make any final determination as to their exact interrelationship.

The Mesopotamian affinities of some of this material, including the astronomical and geographical, seem indubitable. Most recently the possibility has been raised that the apocalypses drew, in this respect, particularly on the widespread mantic or oracular wisdom of ancient Mesopotamia. This was a tradition of learning associated with a particular class of wise men. Its chief subject was the interpretation of dreams and omens, and some associated matters. This sort of context seems particularly helpful when we come to study a figure like Daniel. Astronomy was subordinated to astrology, too, in Mesopotamia, and the Mesopotamian character of the astronomical lore of the *Book of Enoch* has been remarked upon.

Another possible tributary feeding into this stream is the priestly interest in the sacred calendar and the heavenly Temple. Yet a third point of view, less soundly based, points to the Israelite schools of didactic wisdom. The difficulty with this is that there is no evidence that these were concerned with the sort of speculative material being discussed here. Whatever the sources be, one thing is clear; no tradition, literary type or specific group can be identified in the biblical sources, which fostered this type of speculative wisdom. It does not necessarily follow that this sort of interest was imported from abroad into third century Judaism. If there were foreign elements in it, it is still difficult to tell how long they had been there before this material finally surfaced in the preserved sources.

In any case, an additional stage in the development of the apocalyptic literature can now be traced. The biblical material which is analogous to the apocalypses may now be termed (with the exception of Daniel) "proto-apocalyptic". A new type of speculative apocalyptic writing is around in the third century, and it does not seem to be directly dependent on the biblical "proto-apocalyptic" texts. This body of material contained some eschatological teachings, but much other material as well. Those apocalypses which stem from the time of the Antiochean persecution and the Maccabean revolt

show the schematizations of history and the shift of eschatological belief to that which will henceforth typify this literature.
Certain apocalypses which are difficult to date but which
probably stem from the time before the destruction of the
Second Temple in the year 70 C.E., are now more easily
understood, since they have much more of the speculative
material in them than do the works of the time of the Maccabean uprising. In them an old interest of the apocalypses is
again to the fore. A final body of writings stemming from the
period after the destruction of the Second Temple form a
separate, distinct type, distinguished by their preoccupation
with the problem of theodicy, formulated in highly theological
terms. Their central concern is to understand how God's
justice evinces itself in the world, particularly in view of the
destruction of Jerusalem and of the Temple.

6

THE SOURCES AND OUR VIEW OF REALITY

Our last observations have looked forward into the period from the early second century on. Some of the implications of the early date of parts of the *Book of Enoch* bear upon the study of this period. But before we go on to examine this rather exciting age in Jewish creativity, we must reconsider the problem of the sources and their transmission. The study of the time after 200 B.C.E. encounters a difficulty quite different from that relating to the period down to that date. Instead of having only the canonical literature, the historian of this period is presented with a great multiplicity of sources; the problems are those of the presuppositions by which these sources are evaluated and the picture of Judaism resulting from this evaluation.

There were many groups, sects and trends within Judaism before the destruction of the Second Temple. Of these only two survived—Pharisaic Judaism and Christianity. When the sources of this age which were transmitted within the Jewish tradition are examined (i.e. early traditions embodied in rabbinic literature), only a very sketchy picture emerges. It turns out that the rabbinic tradition, the heir of Pharisaic Judaism, preserved relatively little information concerning the period before the destruction of the Second Temple. From such information, it would have been possible to learn that there were various and differing groups within the Jewish community, that some of these differed from the Pharisees, and that others were considered to be *minim* or heretics. There would emerge no realistic idea, however, of that wealth and variety of Judaism which we know existed, but our knowledge of which comes entirely from sources other than rabbinic Judaism.

It was not the practice of ancient religious groups to preserve the opinions, much less the writings of those from whom they differed. And if we are better off in this respect for sources of the history of Judaism in the period following 200 B.C.E. than for the preceding centuries, it is because many such sources were preserved outside the "canonical" Jewish tradition. The chief context in which such extra-canonical Jewish writings were preserved was the Christian church. As Christianity spread throughout the east (and eventually the west), first sacred scriptures, and then other interesting writings, came to be translated into the languages used by the Christians, primarily Greek and Syriac, but subsequently Latin, Coptic, Ethiopic, Armenian, Georgian, Arabic, Old Church Slavonic, and others.

This turns out to have been a very fortuitous development. The vagaries of the transmission of writings from the ancient world are strange. While some of the Apocrypha and Pseudepigrapha might have been considered objectionable by the Rabbis on grounds of content, in many other cases this was not so. Yet none of these books were preserved in the Hebrew or Aramaic original by the Jewish tradition. The reason for their disappearance is not known. Many of these books were translated into Greek. The Apocrypha, of course, were preserved (except for the Fourth Book of Ezra = 2 Esdras) as part of the Greek Bible. Why certain of the Pseudepigrapha were lost in Greek, while others survived, is a subject of speculation in the present state of our knowledge. But where the Greek is lost, then the survival of the book in one of the translations made from the Greek has often rescued it from oblivion. A great deal remains to be done on the question of why certain writings are preserved in a given Christian tradition and others not. All these sources, however, may rightly

be regarded as lying outside the Jewish tradition of transmission.

By way of reminder: if we were dependent on the rabbinic
sources alone, we would know very little about the Maccabean
revolt and very little about the war against the Romans in
68–70 C.E. A good deal is known about the former because of
two books which are preserved in Greek—one a translation
from Hebrew—these are the two Books of Maccabees. A great
deal is known about the details and the course of the war
against the Romans because the writing of the Jewish historian,
Flavius Josephus, survived in Christian hands. Without his
histories, written in the last decades of the first century C.E.,
our knowledge of the first revolt would be as fragmentary
and sketchy as is our knowledge about the second revolt,
that under Bar Kochba, half a century later. Or again, had
the Christian church not preserved the writings of the Alexandrian Jewish philosopher, Philo Judaeus (25 B.C.E.–50
C.E.), this first major attempt to achieve a theological expression of Judaism using the conceptual instruments formulated by Greek philosophy would have remained unknown.
The whole of Jewish writing in Greek, which was rather
extensive at this time, would have been completely lost,
except perhaps for knowledge of the fact that the Bible had
been translated into Greek. Virtually all these sources were
preserved by the Christian churches alone.

In the areas of archaeology, too, the historian of Judaism of
the period after the Maccabean revolt has been more fortunate
than his confrère of an earlier period. The discovery of the
Dead Sea Scrolls has been a find of major importance, and
their extensive implications will be discussed below. For the
moment it is enough to observe that one of the chief contributions of the Scrolls to the historian of Judaism lies in the fact
that they illumine a type of Judaism whose existence no one
guessed. Inscriptions, too, have been more rewarding for
this period than for earlier ages.

Thus, for the period of time after the Maccabean revolt,
the variety and multifaced nature of Judaism has been un-

covered, thanks to those sources which were preserved outside the orthodox Jewish tradition of rabbinic literature. It is only the epigraphic material of all these later sources which is in the Hebrew or Aramaic languages. The other documents, preserved by Christianity, are all extant only in translations. Thus, to the usual problems which any historian faces in the interpretation of ancient documents, are added those which arise from the fact that the documents are translations whose originals have perished.

Particular problems arising in the study of translations include the following. First, the original text of the translation must be recovered (or as much of it as possible) by application of the methods of textual criticism. Next, if possible, the character of the translation must be determined. It is important to know whether the translation is an accurate and faithful one, or whether it is periphrastic; whether it is literal or a polished literary production. If the text from which the translation was made (usually the Greek) has perished without a trace and there are no other versions of the book with which comparison may be made, then this determination is difficult and can only be made, if at all, after a careful study of the translation techniques used in other texts in that language, which are better attested. Most often, however, some of the Greek has survived, even if only in fragmentary form. Nonetheless, the vagaries of translation add to the difficulties of interpretation and, if the original text is missing, it is often difficult to tell what came from the pen of the author and what is a later addition or interpretation by a scribe or copyist, either conscious or unconscious.

In spite of this, the varieties of Jewish religious literature and expression that can be found in the sources preserved only outside the Jewish tradition are notable and important. However, it should immediately be observed that the selective preservation of sources was by no means the exclusive prerogative of the Jews. If all that we know of Judaism was the information preserved in Christian sources, then major dimensions of Judaism would not be known at all and the presentation of other parts of it sadly distorted.

It is evident, therefore, that the understanding and view that we have of Jewish history of the age of the Second Temple are conditioned by these two main factors—the presuppositions of historiography and the character of the sources. There is an intimate relation between these two which should be further explored. Clearly, the nature of the sources which have been transmitted in both the Jewish and Christian traditions has been determined by the particular varieties of Judaism and Christianity which became "orthodox", or in other words, which became dominant and survived.

Judaism and Christianity both rejected material which was not in agreement with their understanding of the past and of themselves. Yet these orthodoxies, both Jewish and Christian, only became established as such after the period which we are discussing. This means that the material they preserved about the age that interests us is that which was acceptable through the filter of orthodoxy. In no case were unorthodox works preserved for the sake of research, study or the like. But the filter of orthodoxy is more pervasive than this, for most of the scholars working on the task of delineating Judaism of the "pre-orthodoxy" period are themselves working from the presuppositions of the later orthodoxies. They tend to emphasize and study those aspects of Judaism of the period of the Second Temple which were important for the development of the later Jewish or Christian orthodoxies, or for the exegesis of the scriptures of those later orthodoxies. Thus Jewish scholars tend to emphasize those features of the Jewish literature and thought of the period of the Second Temple which found resonances in rabbinic literature and in talmudic writings. Works by Jewish scholars have been devoted predominantly to the *halachic* (Jewish legal) aspects of the documents, to their relationship to midrashic traditions and the like.

Equally one-sided have been the Christian treatments of these writings. In them two factors were at work. First, as the Jewish scholars did for rabbinic sources, they sought those features of the Second Temple period Judaism which were directly relevant to the understanding of the New Testament or of early Christianity. There are endless studies, for example, on Jewish Messianism in the period of the Second Temple. A subject such as the term "Son of Man" in the *Book of Enoch* must have had tens of studies devoted to it, not because of the intrinsic importance of this concept, but because it is the closest Jewish parallel to the New Testament term. Indeed, the subject is still under active discussion.

This point should be further clarified: we do not deny the appropriateness of studying Judaism of the period of the Second Temple in order to find information which might help elucidate this or that matter in the New Testament. This is, in itself, a quite proper and, indeed, a necessary procedure. The New Testament was written in that period, and the first body of literature with which it should be compared is the contemporaneous literature of other Jewish groups than the early Christians. The point is that this procedure becomes misleading when the exegetical task is confused with the historical. For example, it is quite appropriate to find illuminating parallels to New Testament Messianic expectations in contemporary Jewish writing. To use the sorts of questions that one might ask in the course of that task, or the sort of criteria it might lead one to apply to the sources, in order to describe Jewish eschatological hopes of the same period, might well be misleading. It is quite possible that those views and those traditions which became embodied in the New Testament were central to all Jewish future expectation. It might, however, equally be the case that they were peripheral to it. Their status and position cannot be determined by the importance of the New Testament for Christianity, but must be discovered by an assembling and evaluation of all the evidence for Jewish eschatology of that age, of which the material contained in the New Testament is part. This is the task for the historian of Judaism. It would, naturally, be equally misleading for him to pursue his labours under assumptions which were determined by the character of rabbinic Judaism in the second or third centuries C.E. Again, a later orthodoxy would have determined the value of the material, the way the evidence is examined and the questions asked of it.

If I seem to labour this point, it is because the task of the historian of Judaism in this period has all too often been abandoned for that of the biblical exegete. It is in this period, nonetheless, that for the first time information is available to the historian which comes from outside the canonical tradition.

There is a second factor which has affected Christian study of Judaism in the age under discussion. This has to do with the attitudes that certain Christians have held towards Judaism, attitudes which have been determined in part by the view that the Church is a new Israel, replacing the old one. What is more, the canonical literature of Christianity was written down at the time when Christianity was still very much involved in its polemic with and its task of self-definition as against Judaism. The result of this has been a negative attitude of many Christian scholars to Judaism, which was based on theological grounds.

Judaism was seen by some of these scholars as a basically negative phenomenon, the stiff-necked perversity of a misguided people who refused in their obstinacy to recognize the quite evident correctness and illumination of Christianity. Such attitudes obviously contributed little to the task of presenting the religious phenomena of Judaism as truly as possible. Moreover, such attitudes permeated the whole of the description of the religious history of the Jews from the time of the First Exile onwards. They are to be found in many influential and basic works of modern biblical and historical scholarship.

Needless to say, the nature of Jewish-Christian relations also affected the way in which Jewish scholars described Judaism. Apologetic tendencies permeate the Jewish writing on the period, and combine with the tendency to read back later orthodoxy into an earlier age. Thus, many Jewish scholars tended to discount those aspects of Judaism in the period of the Second Temple which seemed to run against the rather rationalistic religion of law that they were picturing. It suited this apologetic very well to read back a justified rabbinic

Judaism into the pre-rabbinic age, for many of those features of that earlier age which seemed most like Christianity were thus presented as aberrations in the nature of Judaism.

The motives which led modern scholars of Judaism in the last century (the founders of modern Jewish studies in the tradition of the "Science of Judaism") to present this kind of picture have been analysed by others. They affected the way Judaism was viewed, functioning as criteria for selection in the presentation of the evidence, which was then used to serve ends other than the historian's task of attempting to present the situation as straightforwardly as he can. In the following chapters we shall examine certain aspects of Judaism of this age, from the end of the third century B.C.E. onwards to the first century C.E., which is our focus of interest. The aim will be to transcend, as we can in the light of newer sources, the limited views produced by the earlier state of knowledge.

7

HIDDEN STREAMS IN JUDAISM
Essene Scrolls and Pseudepigrapha

The task now before us is the description of Judaism after 200 B.C.E. in light of two chief factors. The first is the new source material which has become available in recent years, and the second is a reassessment of information from the known sources in light of their transmission and character.

Admittedly, the new discoveries pertaining to the third century B.C.E. do something to soften the sharpness of the contrast between the age of the Restoration (down to 400 B.C.E.) and the period after 200 B.C.E. They have provided some insights into the processes which went on within Judaism and whose fruit appears in the surviving sources in the second century B.C.E. One most prominent characteristic of Judaism of the period after 200 B.C.E. was its fecundity: there grew up an enormous variety of types of Jewish religious expression. This feature of Judaism was part of a general tendency of Hellenistic religious development. In the Hellenistic age pagan religions also underwent deep changes and actively developed new and diverse forms and types of religious expression. They all existed side by side—profound philosophical expressions of religion alongside magic; mystery religions alongside astrology. There developed the cults of gods who promised release from the toils of the body-tomb-world.

The names of numerous groups and sects and trends within Judaism are known from this age—Pharisees and Sadducees, high-priestly families and country folk, Samaritans and

Dositheans, sophisticated Hellenized Jews of the great cities
of the Diaspora, and ascetic, separatist sects like the Essenes.
The number of types and varieties could probably be reckoned
in dozens. As this great range of religious expression is con-
templated, a number of questions and considerations arise to
impose themselves upon us.

First, of all these varieties of Jewish religious expression,
two, or perhaps three, varieties from Judaism have survived.
These are: rabbinic Judaism, Christianity, and perhaps
Samaritanism. Rabbinic Judaism took on its essential form in
the first five centuries of the present era. It is most frequently
associated with the preceding Pharisaic trend in Judaism,
and it is from rabbinic Judaism that all forms of modern
Judaism are descended. The form of Christianity that emerged
triumphant after the struggles of the first two centuries of
Christian existence was but one among many varieties of
Christianity known to have existed from very early days. The
Samaritans today are a group of about 500 souls, some living
still in Shechem (modern Nablus) at the foot of their sacred
Mount Gerizim, and others settled in Holon, near Tel-Aviv.
In ancient and mediaeval times they were a large and active
community, and were also split into a number of sectarian
groups. The other varieties of Jewish religious expression
vanished, some doubtless absorbed by rabbinic Judaism,
others absorbed by Christianity, while yet others fell victim to
the changes of political, social and economic circumstance.

Second, the information we have about these groups does
not, for the most part, stem from rabbinic sources. The rabbis
ignored information concerning groups from which they
differed; or, at best transmitted it in a very incidental fashion.
Virtually nothing would be known of the political fortunes of
the Maccabean dynasty, or of the rebels at Masada from that
source. We would know almost nothing of the Sadducees or
the Essenes in the Judean desert, or of the Jews and Judaism
of the Diaspora. Information about these and many other
groups, sects and trends was transmitted to us from outside the
Jewish tradition. Fortunately, for the historian, Christianity

came from a different part of the spectrum of Judaism from rabbinic Judaism, and therefore its preferences and prejudices were different. As a result, it preserved a very different body of Jewish writing from that which was preserved by the rabbis. Many of the surviving documents of Christianity also came from different parts of the Mediterranean world from those in which rabbinic Judaism developed. Moreover, as already observed, archaeology, too, has been kind to the historian of this age, above all in the remarkable discovery of the Dead Sea Scrolls.

Before we go on to discuss the Dead Sea Scrolls, other sources of information should be considered. One of the first indications of the multifaceted character of Judaism of this age came with the translation into European languages of writings which had been preserved by the various oriental churches, but not by the Greek or Latin ones. The most important at the beginning was the Ethiopic church, but as time went on significant documents were discovered in other oriental languages. Chief among these early translated documents was the *Book of Enoch*. Until recent times, this had been treated as a book witnessing to Judaism in the second and first centuries B.C.E.; and, indeed, three of its five parts were written in those centuries. *The Dream Visions of Enoch* was probably written about the time of the Maccabean revolt, for this extensive political apocalypse refers to Judas Maccabeus. The last part of the *Book of Enoch*, the so-called *Epistle of Enoch*, is more difficult to date, but probably comes from the same period, or even somewhat later. It is our opinion that the *Similitudes of Enoch*, a much-debated group of visions of a heavenly saviour called Son of Man or Elect One, was written in the first century B.C.E. at the latest. The other two parts, we now know, are older. (See above chapters 4–5.)

Another major find of this early period of discoveries was the *Book of Jubilees*. This, like the *Book of Enoch*, was considered to be sacred by the Ethiopic church, and was therefore preserved in full by this church. A partial Latin copy became available somewhat later. The *Book of Jubilees* paraphrases the biblical history from Adam down to Moses, often using the text of the Bible as the basis of its narrative. It is marked by two great peculiarities. It espouses a 364-day solar calendar as the true calendar reckoning, and it promotes certain features of *halachic* (legal) practice which are at variance with other known Jewish law. The 364-day calendar is that which is already advocated by the *Astronomical Book of Enoch*, and was also used by the Dead Sea sect. It must, therefore, have been used in the third century B.C.E., but exactly by whom or for what purpose is unknown. This calendar must have been adjusted somehow to the astronomical year, but we do not know how. The ancient sources mentioned regard this calendar as divinely established, and say that it is in disaccord with the astronomical year because human wickedness has led to a perversion of the natural order. Moreover, the *Book of Jubilees* dates the major events of the patriarchal history by jubilee (49 years), week of years (7 years) and year since creation. The variant *halachic* practice of this book should also be related to that of the Dead Sea sect, although the *Book of Jubilees* probably comes from the period before the separation off of the sect; this aspect of the problem of Qumrân sectarian origins is a matter to which we shall return. The fact that the calendary peculiarities of the *Book of Jubilees* are notably older than the Qumrân sect (see also the *Astronomical Book of Enoch*) indicates that the answers to this problem are complex.

The stimulus provided by these early nineteenth century discoveries of previously unsuspected books, led to further fruitful searches in the libraries of Europe during that century, and to a series of scholarly studies which were much influenced by these works. The name "Pseudepigrapha" has been given to these books, which resemble some of the Apocrypha in general character but are not included in the Latin or Greek Old Testaments. They are Jewish works written in the period of the Second Temple and usually associated with a biblical personality. The first collections of Pseudepigrapha had already been published by J. Fabricius in the eighteenth century, excerpted chiefly from quotations in Greek and Latin patristic authors. The discoveries of the nineteenth century were stimulated by the uncovering of the *Books of Enoch* and *Jubilees* and the exciting vistas these opened before scholars. Such writings as the *Syriac Apocalypse of Baruch*, the Arabic and Ethiopic versions of the *Fourth Book of Ezra* (Second Esdras), the *Books of Adam and Eve* in Latin and Greek and numerous others were published at this time, chiefly from manuscripts housed in the great European libraries. Special studies in the Slavonic apocrypha were stimulated by this development, leading to the publication of versions of a number of writings in Old Church Slavonic, as well as the publication and translation of a few books preserved only in that language. The first collection of Armenian Pseudepigrapha was published at the end of the nineteenth century. M. R. James, an English scholar of wide learning, published many texts and collections of this material from European Greek and Latin manuscripts. Literary detective work still awaits the students of this literature and promises rich results. In a way, the work of the nineteenth century scholarship was summarized in two major collections of the Apocrypha and Pseudepigrapha, one in English edited by R. H. Charles and the other in German edited by Emil Kautzsch.

The type of Judaism which was uncovered by these books differed greatly from those types to which scholars had been accustomed. Many of these writings were very much concerned with eschatological matters, the imminence of the end of days and the way men should act in this last period preceding that end. Moreover, the end of days was not just seen as a chance event, but was understood as having been fixed in advance, as had the whole course of history from creation. In the Bible, the events of history were often regarded as contingent on the actions of men. Israel was told that if its people were righteous, then they would prosper, but if not, then enemies would come upon them and exile and trouble would attend them. As the Jewish Festival liturgy still puts it, "because of our sins we were exiled from our land . . .".

In many of the Pseudepigrapha, however, a determinism

is clearly presented. God fixed the times in advance; they can be calculated (by Him at least); human action is of no weight in determining the course of history. Moreover, these views were conceived under the very strong impression of the dualistic opposition of the world to come and this world. Only in the world to come will the true justice and righteousness of God be revealed, and only in it will the righteous be vindicated. In this world wickedness reigns, "the powers and principalities" control its course. Therefore the righteous, who suffer unjustly in this world, will find their vindication in the world to come. Thus, the course of history is predetermined, and it is predetermined for evil until the end of days. Even more extreme views than these were around, such as those cultivated by the Dead Sea sect, the most extreme of the known Jewish groups to be discussed. The shift from the future hope of the prophets to this sort of eschatological expectation, as we have already seen, may have been precipitated by the sufferings and martyrdoms of the Antiochean persecutions. It became extremely widespread, however, and very influential in all subsequent Jewish and Christian thought.

As distinct from the Dead Sea Scrolls, on the other hand, the Apocrypha and Pseudepigrapha were all writings preserved in living traditions of the various Christian churches. They were brought to bear on the study of Judaism during the nineteenth century, in the period when the historical study of the Bible was becoming separated to some extent from dogmatics, and they worked a revolution in the study of the New Testament. Suddenly they provided insight into a type of Judaism which made certain sorts of interpretation of the Gospels seem particularly plausible, while rendering others obsolete. It was against this background that the interpretation of Jesus as a sort of eschatological preacher arose, and its most influential expression was probably to be found in Albert Schweitzer's famous book, *Quest of the Historical Jesus*. Jewish scholars, on the other hand, did not know how to assimilate this material into their views of the development of Judaism. Clearly much of it stemmed from circles other than the

Pharisaic circles from which rabbinic Judaism had sprung. So the Jewish scholars who approached this material naturally emphasized its legal or *halachic* aspect. They tended to stress those sides of Judaism which the Christian scholars ignored and to deprecate the importance of the extreme eschatological features of these writings.

After the discoveries of the nineteenth century and the publications of the early twentieth century, there was rather a lull in the study of this literature. The stream of scholarship flowed in other channels, and almost nothing was written about many of the Apocrypha and Pseudepigrapha from early in this century until after the Second World War. It took a major archaeological find to turn the attention of scholars once more to the problems of the Jewish literature which has survived outside the Bible and outside rabbinic sources.

The importance of the discovery of the Dead Sea Scrolls in 1947 was manifold. All of the implications of this extraordinary find have not yet been worked out, and they must await the full publication of all the fragments. An assessment of them will be commenced here, but they will recur over and over in the following pages. The actual discovery was of a whole library—fragments of over six hundred manuscripts were found in eleven caves near Khirbet Qumrân, a ruin on a small plateau, a short distance inland from the north-western shore of the Dead Sea. The vast majority of the manuscripts were found in one single cave, Cave 4, where about 400 scrolls had been deposited. The others were found in smaller groups in the ten other caves, with particularly well-preserved manuscripts coming from Caves 1 and 11.

This library had apparently belonged to a Jewish sect who lived in a building near the caves where the manuscripts were discovered. This settlement had existed from the latter part of the second century B.C.E. until 68 C.E. The history of the sect before they settled at Qumrân is little known, except for some fairly obscure references in some of their writings. They apparently split off from the Judaism of Jerusalem some time in the course of or towards the end of the Maccabean revolt.

About twenty years after this a leader arose among them whom they called the Righteous Teacher. He was apparently of priestly descent, and he established, it seems, some of the characteristic patterns of the sect. The Essenes, as they were called, lived at Qumrân continuously, with, perhaps, a break in the time of Herod (37–4 B.C.E.), until its destruction by the Romans in 68 C.E. It was apparently in connection with this destruction that they deposited the manuscripts in the caves. Nothing is known of their history subsequent to the destruction of Qumrân, except for what may be inferred from the discovery of fragments of a sectarian scroll among the ruins of Masada (destroyed in 73 of the present era). This might indicate that some Essenes joined the Zealot camp.

The documents that were discovered at Qumrân can be divided roughly into four groups. The first is manuscripts of the Bible; copies of all parts of the Hebrew Bible have been found at Qumrân, except for the Book of Esther. These are the oldest manuscripts of the Bible, a thousand years older than the next oldest extensive Hebrew manuscripts of any part of the Bible. The second group of manuscripts are copies of certain of the Apocrypha and Pseudepigrapha. These are especially important since these writings were previously known to us only in translation. The very important fragmentary manuscripts of the *Book of Enoch* and the *Testament of Levi* have already been mentioned in Chapter 5. Fragments of other writings, too, were discovered which had been known only in translation. There are, moreover, fragments of a number of compositions which, while they did not survive among the known Apocrypha and Pseudepigrapha, clearly belong to the same class of literature. The third group of manuscripts are those which contain compositions which can be attributed more or less definitely to the Essene sect which inhabited Qumrân. Finally, there are calendary, physiognomic and astrological texts, which perhaps form a sub-class of the third group. The importance of the sectarian writings is that from them can be gained a measure of insight into the religious outlook, customs and habits of a Jewish group quite different in many respects from the rabbinic Judaism which developed out of Pharisaism.

The impact of the Dead Sea Scrolls has been enormous in a whole range of fields of learning. We shall not deal with their ramifications for such matters as the history of the Hebrew language or orthography, of how manuscripts were written, or the like, but instead concentrate on aspects relevant to our general theme. The discovery of these documents in the Semitic original languages was itself of great significance. For the non-biblical books this provided evidence which it was hard for scholars to ignore.

The biblical manuscripts have precipitated a revolution in the study of the text of the Hebrew Bible. They present a complex picture in which various textual types can be found side by side in the one place. The biblical text, like that of any document, underwent change and development. The form of the Hebrew Bible which was preserved by the Jewish tradition is called the Massoretic text. Among the biblical manuscripts from Qumrân there are quite a number that contain a text of this sort. There were, however, at least two other chief textual families in circulation. One is that which underlay an ancient Greek translation of the Bible, the Septuagint. This name means "the Seventy", and it derives from the tradition that the Pentateuch was translated into Greek by seventy or seventy-two elders from Jerusalem at the behest of Ptolemy II Philadelphus (285–246 B.C.E.). What is certain is that the translation of the Pentateuch into Greek was made in the third or early second century B.C.E. and that this was done in Egypt. In a number of biblical books, the text that lay before the translators differed at a number of points from the Massoretic text. The third textual type is that preserved by the Samaritans.

Manuscripts have turned up among the Dead Sea Scrolls that accord with each of these textual types. Incidentally, fragments of the Greek translation of the Bible itself have also turned up among the Qumrân manuscripts, as well as other fragments in Greek. From the occurrence of varied Hebrew

text types at Qumrân it is possible to gain some insight into
a stage of the development of the text of the Hebrew Bible,
preceding the absolute dominance of the Massoretic text.
This latter seems to have come about towards the end of the
first century C.E. Before that there was a multiplicity of
textual types in use which produced a very different situation.

The manuscripts of the Apocrypha and Pseudepigrapha
from Qumrân are important on a number of grounds. From
the preceding discussion of the manuscripts of the *Book of
Enoch*, some aspects of this importance are evident. The
manuscripts aid in dating, in establishing the original language
and as controls over the quality of the translation and the
faithfulness of the transmission. From the manuscripts of the
Aramaic Testament of Levi insight is gained into the growth of
complexes of literary material. Its relationship to the *Greek
Testament of Levi* and the *Book of Jubilees* has already been
discussed (Chapter 5). The manuscripts of the *Book of Tobit*
not only enable us to determine which of the two transmitted
Greek text types has better claim to be original, they also
illustrate the process of translation in the ancient world.
Three of them are in Aramaic (apparently the original) and
another in a Hebrew translation made from it. Moreover, the
discovery of other similar works widens the body of primary
sources at our disposal, although it should be stressed that
the vast majority of the Qumrân manuscripts are rather
fragmentary in character and that the publication of many of
the fragments has not yet been achieved.

For the historian of Judaism perhaps the most interesting of
all of these groups of manuscripts are those last mentioned.
The sectarian writings are particularly important, since they
have provided much new information. In the area of literature
and literary types, these Qumrân manuscripts provide examples of previously unknown forms. There are many pieces
of hymnic and liturgical literature of which we have no other
examples as early as these. From such writings a view can be
gained of the sect's spiritual attitudes, but their similarity to
other Jewish liturgy which is known from a later age also

highlights the shared and ancient elements here involved. The *pesher* is a sort of biblical commentary in which the inner or secret meaning of the prophetic text is explained. This sort of commentary has almost no parallel elsewhere; it seeks the meaning of the text by a rather fanciful typological sort of exegesis, bearing almost no relationship to the original intent of it. The exegesis usually uncovers secrets, often of the history and future of the sect and sometimes of the whole eschatological process. This shows that the sect saw itself as the true community of Israel to whom the secret meaning of the prophetic word applied. What is more, this sort of exegesis of the text as a revelation of secrets seems to be limited, in the extant sources from the period of the Second Temple, to the Qumrân sectarian documents.

Another literary type limited to Qumrân in the present state of information is the *serekh* or "order". We have a number of documents bearing this title, and they are all prescriptive writings, designed to show and instruct on correct conduct. One of them, the *Order of the Community*, gives the regulations for the initiation of new members into the sect, and of their daily life. Another gives the regulations for conduct of the communal meals of the Essenes. Yet another, the *War of the Sons of Light against the Sons of Darkness*, which was probably entitled the *Order of War*, sets forth in immense detail the predetermined course of the great war which is destined to take place at the end of days.

These sectarian scrolls have provided details of points of view which, before their discovery, would never have been considered to be Jewish. The Dead Sea covenanters lived under a strong feeling of the imminence of the end. This eschatological tension was so high that they felt that their own community lived in a sort of anticipation or prolepsis, a bridging as it were of the gap between this age and the age to come. They were the plantation of saplings which was destined, at the end, to become a forest of great trees. They carried on a communal mode of life controlled by a strictly hierarchical organisation. Entry into the sect was carefully regulated, and the postulant passed through a process of careful examination which lasted for some years. Together with the eschatological tension which underlay their life, and the stringent demands made on members of the sect in the fields of morals and conduct, the group was strongly *halachic* in character and orientation. The chief administration of these matters was in the hands of the hereditary priests, the sons of Aaron. Indeed, their *halacha* was much stricter in many respects than that of the Rabbis.

The sect's theology was strongly dualistic and deterministic. The dualism was not simply between this world and the world to come, but was based on an utter opposition between good and evil which were separated and in conflict on both the earthly and heavenly levels. The angelic world was divided into two, as was the world of men—the righteous were led by the angel of light and the wicked by the angel of darkness. Men were predetermined to be in one or the other of these two groups or lots from before their birth. The times of the world too were fixed in advance, and this age was to conclude in a great battle between the forces of light and those of darkness. This battle was to take place both on a this-worldly level and in the cosmic sphere. Angels and demons, the children of light and the children of darkness, Israel (= the sect) and the nations would be locked in a combat whose outcome was, in fact, determined in advance.

This sort of point of view is, of course, strongly opposed to that of the Pharisees. Josephus gives us the basic information we possess about the four chief Jewish sects of this period. From his account and from the rabbinic sources it seems that the Pharisees opposed the dualistic determinism of the Dead Sea sect. They held, instead, that man is endowed with free will, that the choice between good and evil is the responsibility of the individual; that each human being is endowed with moral responsibility. Had the Dead Sea Scrolls not been discovered, it is difficult to say whether the existence of views such as those the Essenes held, would have been thought to be plausible within the framework of Judaism.

As stated above, it seems most likely that others besides those who lived at Qumrân were influenced by this wing of Jewish religion. The evidence of the existence of certain of the characteristic features of the Qumrân sect's ideology in the third and early second centuries B.C.E. has already been assembled in Chapter 4. It includes adherence to the 364-day calendar, the use of certain sorts of terminology to refer to the group under consideration, and some other features of religious ideas. Such groups or such a wing of Judaism must have continued in existence during the second century—in general, such groups were responsible for most of the parts of the *Book of Enoch*. Other products of such groups are the *Book of Jubilees*, and some of the documents underlying the *Testaments of the Twelve Patriarchs*.

Most of the relevant parts of the *Book of Enoch* and also the *Book of Jubilees* originated from before the period in which the Qumrân scrolls were written, but they share technical vocabulary with them, and also calendar. Thus, it seems that the Qumrân sect developed from a wing of Judaism that had been around in the third century. The occurrence of extensive calendarical and astrological texts at Qumrân, as well as physiognomic documents (telling men's character from their physiognomic characteristics) and descriptions and measurements of the heavenly Temple, together with historical narratives structured by Jubilees (49 year periods)—all these hint at connections with the sorts of circles which were responsible for the production of the third century speculative and pseudo-scientific texts. After all, the manuscripts of the *Book of Enoch* were preserved and copied by the Dead Sea sect. Such tendencies as these seem to have taken on a separatist, sectarian complexion in the course of the second century.

There is clear evidence in the historical sources that the people who lived at Qumrân were not the only type of Essenes. Josephus refers to different groups of Essenes, and some of them, according to his account, lived in villages and cities throughout the land (Josephus, *War* 2.124–125). The *Damascus Document*, found first in the Cairo Geniza, is an indubitably sectarian writing, and its connection with the Essenes is clearly shown by the discovery of fragments of it among the Dead Sea Scrolls. It provides, among a number of interesting matters, rules for sectaries who lived not in a chief communal centre, such as that at Qumrân, but in smaller groups (called "camps"). This may be seen as corroboration of Josephus' statements. Moreover, some difficult passages in the sectarian scrolls seem to refer to a migration of the sect (or part of it) to the "land beyond Damascus". The impact of Essene-type ideas on some parts of the New Testament also witnesses to the spread of views analogous to those of the Qumrân folk in the first century C.E.

8

SECTS, TEMPLES AND THE OCCULT

In the preceding chapter some aspects of the contribution which the Dead Sea Scrolls have made to the study of Judaism in the second and first centuries B.C.E. were examined. The importance of this find is not only in the wealth of new data it makes available, but also in the fact that it can be connected with a specific group of people, living and acting at a specific time. The relationship between the archaeological remains at Khirbet Qumrân and the caves containing the scrolls seems assured. The dating of the destruction of the communal buildings seems certain at the year 68 C.E., and their foundation was late in the second century B.C.E. The identification of the sectaries with the Essenes seems certain, both on the basis of Pliny's location of the Essene community (*Historia Naturalis* 5.15.73) which seems to refer to Qumrân, and of Josephus' description of their way of life, which agrees substantially with the regulations found in the *Order of the Community*, also known as the *Manual of Discipline* (especially *War* 2, 119–161).

Such precision of dating, location or identification of documents is without parallel in other Jewish trends and sects of the same age. Josephus, in two extensive passages, provides us with descriptions of the Jewish sects of his time (*War.* 2.119–166; *Antiquities* 18:11–22). He identifies four "philosophies", the three chief ones being the Pharisees, the Sadducees and the Essenes. The so-called "fourth philosophy" he states to be the Zealots, an activist group which was particularly prominent in the events leading up to and surrounding the revolt against the Romans in 68–70 C.E. In his description of the Essenes he goes into considerable detail and provides interesting corroboration for the material now available from the Dead Sea manuscripts. On the other hand, his descriptions of the Pharisees and the Sadducees are rather summary, concentrating on certain specific matters.

In addition to the information which is to be gained from Josephus, there are a number of additional sources which provide us with scraps of knowledge about these groups. These additional sources include one or two documents from among the Dead Sea Scrolls, particularly the *Commentary on Nahum* from Cave 4. The New Testament provides some information about and insight into the attitudes that prevailed among the various groups. There is also something to be learned about the situation before the destruction from rabbinic writings, but none of these sources is particularly rich or detailed. Additional information on the Essenes is to be found in the writings of Philo of Alexandria (25 B.C.E.–50 C.E.), and he also discusses in detail the characteristics of another Jewish sect which existed in Egypt, the Therapeutae, who are the chief subject of his treatise *On the Contemplative Life*. Still other groups are known to have existed, and these are mentioned in one or more sources.

In addition to the historical reports and occasional snippets we have mentioned, our primary sources for the study of Jewish thought and religious ideas in the period under discussion are the books of the Apocrypha and Pseudepigrapha. It is exactly at this point that one of the chief differences between these books and the Dead Sea Scrolls becomes apparent. While the latter can be clearly located in time, place and society, the Apocrypha and Pseudepigrapha are very different. We do not know for certain by whom the vast majority of them were written, or for whom, or often even when. The books were preserved by Christians and, because of their literary character, they do not transmit historical information; the vast majority of them are not histories. So the location of the composition of the books in society and time becomes a complex matter. Occasionally, careful scholarly study and investigation, together with the use of internal criteria or external ones, such as quotations or allusions in positively dated authors, can help us to date them. It is very much more difficult, however, to place these writings within the complex of society and the variety of social groups of whose existence we learn through study of the historical works.

This difficulty is compounded by the fact that we have almost no clearly attributed writings with which the Apocrypha and Pseudepigrapha can be compared. Nothing at all survives which was written by one of the two chief groups, the Sadducees. Some traditions and teachings may exist in rabbinic sources which go back to Pharisaic masters before the destruction of the second temple. These are, however, chiefly legal in character and do not provide any suitable material which can be used to place the various documents of the Apocrypha and Pseudepigrapha. One sole fragment of Samaritan literature of early date is preserved, and that only in Greek.

The Pharisees and Sadducees appear on the stage of history in the latter part of the second century B.C.E. Prior to that time the Books of Maccabees mention the Hasideans, but the amount of information on them is very small indeed. Some have suggested that both the Essenes and the Pharisees were groups that developed out of the Hasideans during and after the Maccabean revolt. The Hasideans are not heard of again after they abandoned the Hasmonean cause in the mid-second century. Others have suggested that the Hasideans continued to exist down into the first century, and that they may have been connected with the group of "pious of old" *(hasidim rishonim)* mentioned by the early rabbinic sources. This may be so, but there is no evidence to show it and, at most, the "pious of old" may be regarded as yet another of the rather numerous groups whose existence is known. They are spoken of with approval by the Rabbis and may have been close to "proto-rabbinic" circles. The importance of the Dead Sea Scrolls is thus clear, for they enable us to place the Essenes in the context of their writings, and we can thus isolate a whole wing or type of Judaism of whose existence we were previously ignorant.

The Pharisees and Sadducees play a major role in Josephus' narrative of the events in Judea. The Pharisees are characterized, above all, as exegetes of the scriptures, marked out by skill in this activity and by the authority with which they regard their own exegesis. This chief feature also comes to the fore in the description of them in the *Commentary on Nahum* from Qumrân. There they are called the "smooth exegetes", and this same aspect of Pharisaic teaching is to the fore at many points in the New Testament. Incidentally, it should be observed that the accounts both in the Essene documents and in the Christian ones are rather hostile to the Pharisees, while Josephus regards them as the primary group and is favourable towards them. They differed from the Sadducees on a number of grounds—their attitude to the exegesis of scripture, to divine providence, to a future life and to angelology. Josephus' picture of the Sadducees is one of a somewhat different social class to the Pharisees—they were far more aristocratic in character, connected with the priestly upper classes and the wealthy. The *Commentary on Nahum* from Qumrân presents a consonant view of the Sadducees.

Clearly, in the long run, it was the attitude to the Torah and the modes of exegesis which the Pharisaic teachers developed that provided Judaism with the instruments by which the terrible trauma of the destruction of the Temple in the year 70 C.E. might be overcome. By providing a system of exposition which permitted them to adapt and develop the principles of Pentateuchal legislation, they were able to create the necessary structures and patterns of life to respond to the needs of that hour. Their system of law and exegesis has shown its continued vitality as a religious world view throughout subsequent generations.

There is a good deal of information yet untouched by our survey which should be brought within our purview. Recent studies have assembled evidence from archaeological and historical sources to raise intriguing questions on attitudes to the temple in Jerusalem. Since this was the central institution of Jewish religious life, the attitudes to it are of importance for understanding the Judaism of the age with which we are dealing.

The *Aramaic Testament of Levi* expresses the hope that at the end of days a priestly Anointed One will come to restore the true constitution of Israel (see Chapter 5). Of course, the primary element of such restorative expectations was that of the coming Anointed One, descendant of King David, who would re-establish the Davidic monarchy. Among the Dead Sea Scrolls there are a number of texts which express the hope of the future coming of two Anointed Ones, of Aaron and of Israel, or the priestly and the royal. This expectation is also to be found in certain passages of the Greek *Testaments of the Twelve Patriarchs*.

In this modification of the messianic hope, in fact an old pattern was coming to the fore—a pattern which had existed from the Persian period at least. From that time on the priesthood had held pride of place in Judean society. Judah was a temple state and the High Priest was its chief official. Two centuries later, in the sad events which led up to the Antiochean decrees, it was the High Priesthood that was the bone of contention between the various aspirants to power. Eventually, at that time, the Zadokite family was displaced from its hereditary position and the last Zadokite High Priest (Onias III) fled to Egypt. When Simon the Hasmonean assumed the High Priesthood it was as a provisional measure until the true line was restored. When he took the position of Ethnarch as well he reunited the two central offices in his person (141 B.C.E.).

There seems to be a good reason to think that the Essenes broke away and became a sectarian community because of their opposition to the expulsion of the Zadokite line from the

High Priestly office. For them, the Restoration and its temple were not reckoned as having taken place, and they regarded themselves as still in exile. In other words, their reverence for the temple was such that the rejection of the legitimacy of the priesthood made them sever themselves from the body of Israelite Society. Indeed, there are texts which show that the Dead Sea sectaries, like the Christians who were to follow them, regarded their community as the temple or as Jerusalem. In this they were carrying to an extreme the expectation of an ideal Jerusalem and a tendency towards the spiritualization of cult which may be discerned in texts from the third pre-Christian century onwards.

The pattern of Anointed of Aaron and Anointed of Israel has roots going back at least into the fifth century B.C.E. The prophet Zechariah saw the vision of two olive branches, which are Joshua the High Priest and Zerubbabel ben Shealtiel, the descendant of David (Zech chap.4). Half a millennium later, on the coins of Bar Kosiba, who regarded himself and was regarded as the expected son of David, a certain Eleazar the Priest is also mentioned. In between, this dual expectation was nurtured in groups such as the Essenes. The true restoration of Israel was the double one of restoration of High Priest and King, of the son of Aaron and the son of David.

All of this evidence serves to illustrate the central place of the temple in Jerusalem in the life of the Jewish people, as long as it still stood. The sacrificial cult and the priests who carried it out were endowed with the special sanctity. The major role of the Jerusalem temple must go back to the time of its establishment by Solomon, but its exclusive position as the only place where the sacrificial cult of God was carried on is usually attributed to the reforms of King Josiah, which are assumed to have commenced in 621 B.C.E. At that time, it would appear from the Book of Kings, that a systematic attempt was made to do away with all cult centres outside Jerusalem, and to permit the sacrificial cult only at the single sanctuary in Jersusalem.

The central position of the Jerusalem temple thenceforth

scarcely needs documentation. It is enough to recall that its rebuilding was the chief aspiration of those who returned from the Babylonian exile; the dismay and distress at its desecration by Antiochus Epiphanes, and later by Pompey, are eloquent witnesses to this centrality. The attitudes to the temple of the early second century sage, Jeshua ben Sira, are eloquently expressed in the 49th chapter of his book, his description of the awesome and beautiful appearance of the Zadokite High Priest Simon. Rabbinic sources are unanimous that the temple in Jerusalem is the one permissible cult centre of the Jewish people.

For the Jews of the Diaspora, too, the temple played a very special role. The fact of very extensive Jewish settlement outside the land of Israel is one of the central characteristics of Jewish life in the Second Temple period. The scattering of the Jews had begun in the eighth century with the exile of the Northern kingdom of Israel by King Sargon of Assyria (722–721 B.C.E.). Then there were repeated deportations to Mesopotamia during the early sixth century B.C.E., while simultaneously we hear of Jews, including the prophet Jeremiah, moving to Egypt. In the fifth century B.C.E. there were Jewish mercenary soldiers in Upper Egypt. From that time the Diaspora seems to have grown, and some estimates place in millions the number of Jews living outside the land of Israel by the first century B.C.E. Philo refers to a million Jews in Alexandria alone at that time.

For these Jews of the Diaspora the temple in Jerusalem became a central national symbol and institution. During the last pre-Christian centuries, we hear of a developing custom of pilgrimages from the Diaspora which, together with the temple tax paid by every Jew all over the world, served as an important bond between the Jews of the Diaspora and the national institutions in Jerusalem. In all of this the temple played the chief role.

Yet, throughout the period from the sixth century B.C.E. on, we hear also of a series of Jewish temples outside Jerusalem. Excavations have uncovered a temple at Arad, near Beer-

Sheva, surviving the Josianic reforms, patterned exactly on the Jerusalem sanctuary. In the fifth century B.C.E. the Jews of Elephantine had a temple in their Upper Egyptian colony. A number of papyrus letters and documents emanating from this colony have been uncovered. These are written in the Aramaic language and provide some insight into the way of life of these Jewish soldiers and their relationships with their neighbours.

One of the documents is a copy of a letter which the Jews of Elephantine sent to the Persian governor of Judah in the year 408 B.C.E. Another copy went to the Samarian Governor's sons. In it they relate that their temple has been burned down in a pogrom and appeal for assistance in rebuilding it. There are a number of points of interest for us in this document. The first is that the Jews of Elephantine had a temple, and that when it was destroyed they felt no compunction about appealing to the governors of Judah and Samaria to help in its rebuilding. From this it may be inferred that they felt their temple to be quite unexceptionable and legitimate. Secondly, they appeal to the governors of both Judah and Samaria. This serves to remind us that, from the Hellenistic period, there was also a Temple of the God of Israel in Shechem. This particular group of Jews appealed equally to both. Thirdly, the cult which was carried on in their temple, as can be inferred from the papyri, seems to have been of God, together with other associated deities; in other words, some kind of syncretistic cult. This first insight into Jewish religious life from extra-biblical sources provides some surprises.

There are those who would discount the importance of the Elephantine community, as not typical of Jewish life. They would maintain that the people of Elephantine had stemmed from the area of the northern kingdom of Israel, and that their syncretistic cult and willingness to have a temple outside Jerusalem may be attributed to their having escaped the Josianic reforms altogether. Other scholars would maintain that the Elephantine Jews had assimilated pagan customs and practices during their many years of service with the Persian army. Both these hypotheses may be true, but neither is particularly persuasive. What is undubitably true is that the temple in Elephantine is just one of a number of Jewish temples which are known to have existed outside Jerusalem, indeed outside the land of Israel, during the period of the Second Temple. Thus, even if one maintains that the Jews of Elephantine were some sort of deviant group, such an opinion should be based on their syncretistic cult and not on the fact that they had a temple.

Another temple, this time dating back to the second century B.C.E., was unearthed about twenty years ago in Transjordan, at a site called Araq el-Emir. This temple structure was apparently never completed. Its building was commenced by a certain Hyrcanus, who was a member of the Tobiad family (early second century B.C.E.). This varonial clan is known to us from the writings of Josephus. From them we learn that the Tobiads rose to particular prominence in the third century B.C.E. under the Ptolemaic rule, but that their power continued down into the second century B.C.E. Earlier they had been the tax-farmers for the whole of Judah. After certain political events, this Hyrcanus withdrew from Jerusalem, and it seems that he made his centre at Araq el-Emir. There he proceeded to erect a building which, on grounds of its architectural qualities, can definitely be identified as a temple. It might be added that the Tobiads were intermarried with the High Priestly family in Jerusalem, and therefore may be presumed to have been quite familiar with attitudes surrounding the temple in Jerusalem.

The connection of the builder of the next temple to be mentioned with the Jerusalem temple is even less in doubt. He was the son of Onias III, the last of the Zadokite High Priests, who was deposed by Antiochus IV Epiphanes in 175–174 B.C.E., and fled to Egypt. This was early in the course of the intrigues which eventually led to Antiochus' imposition of the decrees against the Jewish religion. His son, Onias IV, with the permission of Antiochus' Ptolemaic rival, proceeded to build a temple and found a military colony at a

place called Leontopolis, in the vicinity of Alexandria. Very
little indeed is known about the history of this sanctuary
after its foundation about 160 B.C.E., and no information
has survived concerning its cult, circle of adherents and the
like. It has been suggested that certain of the Jewish writings
in Greek which stem from Egypt were written there, but this
remains speculative. Josephus relates that the Romans
eventually closed this temple as a precaution, soon after their
destruction of the temple in Jerusalem in the year 70 C.E. It
seems difficult to maintain that the son of the Zadokite High
Priest of the temple in Jerusalem was not aware of the commonly accepted single-sanctuary view. Yet it is clear that he
did not feel it to be so binding as to prevent his undertaking
the building of another temple outside the land of Israel.
Moreover, Josephus feels nothing strange about it, or at least
betrays no opinion of its unusual character: and it is worth
recalling that Josephus, too, was a priest. The Dead Sea sect
may have made animal sacrifices at Qumrân, since it rejected
the Jerusalem Temple, carefully buried animal bones, and
Josephus so asserts (*Antiquities* 18:19).

Josephus preserves one further account (similar to the
above) of a Jewish sacrificial cult outside Jerusalem, in his
Antiquities of the Jews. In that work he transcribes a proclamation made by the *boulē*, that is the governing body, of the city
of Sardis in Asia Minor in the time of John Hyrcanus II
(63–40 B.C.E.). The proclamation permits the Jews to establish their cult in the city. The word used for cult is the Greek
term *thysia*, which some scholars have wished to interpret in a
general way as "gifts", or "offerings". Yet, this is not the way
this word developed. It normally means an animal sacrifice,
and it develops in secular contexts in the direction of "slaugh-
tering of animals, not necessarily for cultic purposes". Thus,
in the decree of the *boulē* the word specifically denoted sacrificial cult, and that is what the Jews of Sardis were permitted
to establish. It is, of course, possible that this statement reflects misunderstanding by the Sardis Council of Jewish ritual
activity. At the least, its bald report in Josephus is strange.

Thus, from the sixth century B.C.E. onward there existed a number of Jewish temples inside and outside the land of Israel, but all of them apart from the Temple in Jerusalem. This went on throughout a period in which the central position of the Temple in Jerusalem was in no doubt whatsoever. What is the meaning of this evidence, to which a number of further items might be added? Each case could be modified or argued away on grounds some of which have been indicated above. Taken as a whole, however, this evidence demands our attention and consideration, for it is quite impressive. The initial issue is how it fits with the well known and generally accepted view that Jerusalem alone had rights to the temple of God. This claim is explicit in biblical Scriptures, and had been established for centuries by the time Hyrcanus and Onias built their temples, and the Jews of Sardis petitioned the *boulē*. The situation is, after all, rather surprising, for the claims of the sources from the Books of Kings on are quite unambiguous. Are these claims not a statement of the situation, but merely the tendentious presentation as fact of what was actually the wishful thinking of the authors? This would be an extreme conclusion to draw.

Yet clearly something is going on, and it does seem to be the case that the biblical sources do not present a complete view of what was considered permissible by certain circles, some of which were very close to the priesthood of the temple in Jerusalem is unambiguous, even in those very documents variety of viewpoint than the biblical sources indicate. At the same time much of the evidence is from a much later period than the Book of Kings, and the central position of the temple in Jerusalem is unambiguous, even in those very documents which report that there were other temples outside Jerusalem. So, it seems that the attitudes to the exclusive rights of Jerusalem were less absolute than had been thought.

This body of evidence indicates that we must maintain a more complex view of the character of Judaism than might otherwise have been thought necessary. Even the temple, which was clearly the central common institution around whose sanctity the vast majority of the Jewish people united, was in fact subject to differing attitudes. In its case, the major evidence which contradicts the picture presented by the written sources comes from archaeological discoveries—the Elephantine papyri, the ruins of Araq el-Emir among others. Presented with these, we are moved to reassess certain pieces of evidence which we have in the written sources, chiefly that of Josephus. This reassessment is carried out in the light of new questions which the archaeological discoveries raise. It is in processes like this that new advances are made in historical description. Very often much of the evidence was present all along, but its interpretation is new.

Another body of evidence which serves to complicate the picture of Judaism at this period relates to Jewish magic and magicians. In general, the Hellenistic age was characterized by an interest in the occult, and magic played a great role in the world of that time. The Jews, it seems, were prominent among the magicians of this era, and there were considerable Jewish elements in Graeco-Roman magic. It is true, of course, that the magical or manipulative is an element present in every religion, yet the written records of Judaism seem fairly consistent in their strong condemnation of magic. Even in a sectarian document like the *Book of Enoch*, magic is reckoned among the wicked teachings transmitted by the fallen angels. They revealed it to the daughters of men, and its practice is reviled by the *Book of Enoch* as by the Bible. Demon belief and practice of magic were nevertheless widespread.

This situation is evident from the study of many major writings of the period in which reference is made to matters related to magic. Thus, for example, the *Wisdom of Solomon*, a book most probably written in the first century B.C.E. or the first century C.E., tells us that Solomon was granted a great range of knowledge by wisdom. This included "the powers of spirits and the reasonings of men, the varieties of plants and the virtues of roots" (*Wisdom* 8:20). The revelation of the control over the spirit and demonic world was particularly associated with Solomon. So also in a more or less contemporary work, the *Biblical Antiquities* (falsely attributed to Philo), a son of David is prophesied as driving out demons (*Bib.Ant.* 60:2). Josephus records the incident of an Essene who exorcised evil spirits. This he did by passing under the nose of the possessed man a ring upon which Solomon's name was inscribed. Upon this, the demon issued forth from the man's nostrils, Josephus informs us, like thick smoke.

These do not exhaust the witnesses to King Solomon's magical powers. In the somewhat later Greek writing known as the *Testament of Solomon*, it is related that he shackled demons and forced them to help in the building of the temple. The same story recurs with variations in rabbinic legends. Solomon's name occurs on a number of magical signs and amulets of the same general period. In a recently published fragmentary scroll from Qumrân, we also have evidence of this. It contains a chapter of Psalms often used for magical and medical purposes, followed by some very fragmentary columns which repeatedly mention the Hebrew word for demons, and Solomon's name. Of course, in a vast number of later writings and legends Solomon's name is associated with magic and exorcisms in particular.

The *Wisdom of Solomon* also attributes to him the knowledge of plants and the cutting of roots. This hints at a field of knowledge which lay partly in the occult—medicine, and particularly magical medicine. In the *Book of Enoch* 7–8, enchantments and root-cuttings are mentioned together as teachings of Semjaza, who appears in other parts of the work as the chief of the fallen angels; in general terms the angels are said to have taught women "charms and enchantments and the cutting of roots and . . . plants." Thus, the context and meaning of the knowledge of plants and the cutting of roots, which were revealed to King Solomon, are clear.

The medical associations of the use of plants and roots are shown in another interesting document. This is a fragment, apparently, of a lost *Book of Noah*, which is embedded in the *Book of Jubilees* 10:1–14. This text relates how, when Noah left the Ark after the flood, he appealed to God to remove the

demons. The demons had originated from the giants, who were
the offspring of the illicit union of the sons of God with the
daughters of men. Noah prayed to God to remove the demons
and to bind them so that they should not lead the sons of men
astray and afflict them with illnesses. God was about to bind
them all when their prince intervened on their behalf and God
granted that one in ten be left. He also instructed the angels
to transmit to Noah "all the medicines of their diseases, together with their seductions, how he might heal them with the
plants of the earth."

In this text the magical and medical traditions are brought
together, as they very often are in the Hellenistic-Roman
world. This tradition became part of the Jewish medical
learning, for a Hebrew form of this particular part of the *Book
of Jubilees* recurs in the mediaeval Jewish medical composition, the *Book of Asaf the Physician*.

Jewish elements are also to be found in the rather extensive
pagan occult literature of the Hellenistic period, and in the
somewhat later corpus of Greek magical papyri. This connection takes on particular importance because of a recently
published book of Hebrew magical texts. This is the *Sefer
Harazim* or *Book of Mysteries*. It was pieced together from
mediaeval Hebrew manuscripts which survived in the Cairo
Geniza and from parts of the book which were found to be
re-used in later compositions. It contains magical material
and is written in Hebrew and dated by its editor to the third
century C.E. It presents a sort of magical activity which has
its closest analogues in the Egyptian Greek magical papyri.
It is syncretistic in many respects, magic being basically an
international tradition. Typical of the pagan-Jewish mixture
in the *Book of Mysteries* is a prayer to the Greek deity Helios,
composed in Greek and written out in Hebrew letters. The book
contains an ascent text, describing the powers to be found in
each of the heavens and how to manipulate them. The line
between magic and religion is not always as clear as it seems,
and both in the *Book of Mysteries* and in, say, the magical
ascent text in the Paris Magical Papyrus, it is very hard to

draw. Equally complex is the differentiation between certain of the "chariot" texts which involve the invocation of angelic guides and protectors and the invocation of spirit aids in the magical sources.

It seems to be rather significant that, although there was clearly fairly widespread magical activity in the Graeco-Roman world, the apocalypses reject it consistently. The place of secret or revealed information in the apocalypses was central, yet they show no interest in magical or manipulative activity. Indeed, they contain no techniques for the invocation of angels or spirits, and the *Book of Enoch*, for example, condemns magic roundly. At least in the circles that produced these works there was a consistent condemnation of this sort of activity.

Indeed, the apocalypses tell us almost nothing about the ecstatic practice of the seers. Prayer and fasting are mentioned and some have seen significance in the fact that many visions are said to have been received on the banks of bodies of water. There was a magical, meditative technique known from the Graeco-Roman sphere which involved contemplation of a body of water until visions were seen in it. It is conceivable that this may be behind the series of visions received by apocalyptic seers on the banks of rivers or other bodies of water, a tradition going back to *Ezekiel*: chap.1, at least. Yet, one could also argue that most of these cases are using a standard literary element repetitively. Certainly the apocalyptic seers receive no information of a magical character, another indication that such subjects were completely rejected by many circles.

It is, therefore, most probable that the description of Solomon's knowledge in the *Wisdom of Solomon*, chapter 7, is not connected intimately with the apocalypses, but draws upon a particular sort of tradition which associated Solomon with magical activity. In spite of its rejection by the apocalypses, magical activity was prevalent in the Jewish world in the period we are discussing, and this is another of the elements of the Judaism of this age that must be taken into account as we trace the various features which contribute to the picture of this era.

9

HELLENISM AND THE DIASPORA

In the preceding chapter the questions dealt with touched chiefly on the situation in the land of Israel. Now the focus of attention should be directed towards some phenomena of Judaism of the diaspora, the communities that lived outside the land of Israel. As at the present day, so in the period of the Second Temple, the numerical majority of the Jewish people lived outside the land of Israel. In Chapter 8, the historical roots of this dispersion (that is what "diaspora" means) have been indicated, at least in part. Its pattern was already quite old in the Second Temple period, and it has persisted since for more than two millennia. In that period centres of Jewish Diaspora were Egypt (particularly Alexandria), North Africa and Asia Minor, as well as Syria and Mesopotamia to the north and east. There is, moreover, clear evidence of Jewish settlement in a number of other cities and areas, including Greece and the Italian peninsula.

It should also be mentioned that there were centres of Hellenistic Jewry in Jerusalem. Synagogues of various Diaspora communities are mentioned (cf. Acts 6:9), and when the royal house of Adiabene converted to Judaism in the middle of the first century C.E., its members built a major centre in Jerusalem for their graves, the ruins of which survive even today. Rabbinic literature records the visits by eminent rabbis to various parts of the diapora, as well as the despatching of letters from the authorities in the land of Israel to Jews abroad.

Relations between Jewry in the land and those abroad seem to have been quite intimate, but there is also little doubt that there were very real differences between these communities. We have already referred to the impact of Greek systematic thought upon Judaism, particularly diaspora Judaism. Among the great products of this were the philosophical writings of Philo of Alexandria (25 B.C.E.–50 C.E.). This writer, a member of the most eminent family of the great Jewish community of Alexandria, wrote a whole shelf of books, which have mostly survived, thanks to the particular respect with which he was regarded by Christians. He applied to the Bible, especially the Pentateuch, methods of allegorical exegesis that had been developed by the Stoics in their study of Homer. Assuming that the true meaning of divine writings could not be simply to tell the stories of some nomadic tribal ancestors, he systematically allegorized the text of the Bible, seeking in it eternal truths of religious philosophy.

Philo's thought and approach were to have great influence on the school of Christian thought that arose in Alexandria after him. He was not the first thinker, however, to try to express his understanding of Judaism using intellectual instruments drawn from the Greek milieu in which he lived and functioned. The allegorical method freed the biblical text from the stigmata of literalism and anthropomorphism; Philo nonetheless vigorously attacked those who interpret Pentateuchal legislation exclusively allegorically and do not observe its injunctions.

Moreover, apologetics became a major concern of Jewish writers in Alexandria. There were writings in Greek forms, but of Jewish content. Ezekiel the Tragic Poet (date uncertain) wrote a play about the Exodus from Egypt, fragments of which still exist. In this he utilized all of the forms of Greek literary convention for the writing of tragedy, but his subject was Jewish. He was not inhibited from doing this by the fact that the Greek drama was originally a religious activity, devoted to the worship of specific deities. Jewish apologetics went beyond this, however, for Egyptian Jewry took the biblical record and sought in it events and facts which would give a legitimation of their own position in Egypt. In part this may be seen as a reflection of the bitter struggle that went on in Alexandria between the Jewish community and the Greeks (see Josephus, *Against Apion*). So the roles of Joseph and Moses in Egyptian life and society were highlighted. Moreover, a general theme of Jewish writing in Greek was to attribute the foundation of philosophy and of science to the Jewish patriarchs. Plato learned from Moses. Abraham taught astronomy to the Babylonians and, subsequently, to the Egyptians. The patriarchs of the Jewish people had been the founders of learning and civilization.

Perhaps the most extreme of those who presented an *interpretatio graeca* of Judaism was a historian called Artapanus (second century B.C.E.). Throughout the land of Egypt were in fact statues, the statues of the god Sarapis. These, Artapanus claimed, were really statues of Joseph. But that true identity, based on the story reported by Moses, had been forgotten by the Egyptians. His account is syncretistic in other respects also. Joseph is credited with the division of Egypt into districts and its internal organisation, an activity which Greek historians since Herodotus had considered to be the beginning of civilization in Egypt. The Jews in bondage, according to him, built the most marvellous temples in the land of Egypt. Moses is identified with Orpheus' teacher. He is said to have revealed the secrets of hieroglyphic writing and is given some of the characteristics of the Hellenistic wisdom figure Hermes-Thoth. In general, Moses is credited with the invention of the intellectual and technical bases of human culture. Above all, he set up the 36 nomes (administrative districts) of Egypt, each with its own worship. This worship was theriolatry (animal worship) typical of Egypt's cult. Interestingly, in his encomium commonly thought on Moses, which is of clearly apologetic character, Artapanus finds nothing objectionable in attributing to him the foundation of a form of worship which was regarded with abhorrence by Greeks and Jews alike. A similar motif is seen in the single surviving fragment of Hellenistic Samaritan literature, the so-called pseudo-Eupolemus (exact date unknown). He attributes the invention of astronomy to Enoch, whom he identifies with Atlas. Here, not the apologetic element, but the attempt to find an equivalent in Greek mythological tales to the biblical accounts, is to the fore.

There are others who also wrote Jewish literature in the Greek language. Some, like Ezekiel the Tragedian, Artapanus or pseudo-Eupolemus, are known only from fragmentary quotations in later writers. Certain other works have survived in full as part of the Apocrypha and Pseudepigrapha. Nearly all these latter books are written in Jewish literary forms, not Greek. Even the poetry is written in imitation of the style of biblical Hebrew poetry, rather than by the rules of scansion which govern the composition of Greek verse. One such work is the Wisdom of Solomon. This appears to be an Alexandrian composition. It is characterized by some of the apologetic elements also found in other Alexandrian writing (11:15–20; 15:14–16:4). The first part is written in poetic form, but the poetic form is modelled broadly upon prototypes to be found in the Hebrew Bible, not on Greek poetic conventions. This means, of course, that Jews in Alexandria, and perhaps elsewhere in the world, wrote poetry in Greek after biblical models, which indicates the influence which the Greek translation of the Bible must have had among them. Others of the pseudepigrapha are written according to Greek conventions. For example, the *Fourth Book of Maccabees* is in the form of a *diatribe*, that is, a sort of philosophical discourse delivered as a speech, which originated in Cynic philosophical circles. The subject of the book, which was probably also expressed in its original title, concerns the rule of reason (defined as the observance of the Torah) over the passions.

Jews in the Hellenistic diaspora not only had a translation of the Bible into Greek, but also used Greek as a language of liturgy. The measure of knowledge of Hebrew among them must have varied. Philo's acquaintance with Hebrew is much debated, but it seems likely that he did not have a thorough knowledge of the language. By contrast, some of the translations into Greek are extremely competently done, showing a fine command of Hebrew. Others, such as that of the *Epistle of Jeremiah*, are written in extremely poor Greek. A picture emerges of a knowledge of Greek ranging from the rather elementary to the sophistication of Philo or the author of the *Fourth Book of Maccabees*. In the same way, a range of literature appears, from literal translations of Semitic originals to compositions in Greek according to the canons of Greek literature.

It seems reasonable to assume that there was in the greatest likelihood a similar range between piety and assimilation. This must have run all the way from a rather simple, traditional piety to the philosophical religion of people like Philo. There were others whom he attacks who rejected the observance of Judaism in their pursuit of the spiritualizing and allegorical explanations of things; and there were also Jews who were apparently quite assimilated. One such was Philo's nephew, Tiberius Julius Alexander, who was assimilated and made a great career in the imperial service, serving as procurator of Judea in the years 46–48 C.E., and later as governor of Egypt.

By way of conclusion to this part of the discussion, it should be remarked that very little is known of the religious or literary production of any Jewish community in the diaspora outside Alexandria. What is more, if we know little about the Jews in the great centres of the Hellenistic world, it is still incomparably more than we know of the other great area of Jewish diaspora, that of northern Syria and Mesopotamia. All that is known of these are the few details which Josephus communicates and some impressions to be gained from certain of the Apocrypha, particularly the Book of Tobit. Yet this area was to prove extremely important by the third century C.E., for then it was in Mesopotamia that the great centres of Jewish learning arose. This was an Aramaic-speaking Jewry rather than a Greek-speaking one.

It is from Mesopotamia, from the city of Dura Europus, that we have the most remarkable monument of Jewish art from antiquity. This is a synagogue of the third century C.E., whose walls are covered with frescos presenting a variety of Jewish religious scenes drawn primarily from the Bible. Some scholars are of the opinion that these paintings were taken from manuscripts of the Bible of even greater antiquity which were illustrated with pictures. It is a remarkable fact that virtually no figurative art has turned up in Jerusalem and other sites in the land of Israel from the last century B.C.E. and the first century C.E. All that have been found are geometric and architectural types of decoration, some rather elaborate and very well preserved. In some places vegetation and fruit also figure. The reason for the absence of any human figures, and virtually all animal figures, seems to have been a particularly stringent interpretation of the third commandment: "You shall make no graven images".

It would appear then from the rich decoration of the Dura Europus synagogue that the stringent interpretation was not the only way that this commandment could be taken. Indeed, in the coming centuries throughout the land of Israel a remarkable series of figurative representations are found. The most striking are the mosaic synagogue floors. These are covered with representations, often decorative uses of animal or bird motifs, and sometimes more explicit scenes, including pagan deities or pagan representations of natural phenomena. In the rather remarkable catacombs of the Jewish cemetery at Beth Shearim (not far from Haifa) numerous sarcophagi have been found adorned with animal and other figurative representations. So, clearly, the ban on figurative art was relaxed in the early centuries of the present era.

It is not only the Dura Europus frescoes, however, which are thought to have been drawn from illustrated Bible manuscripts. Studies of illustrated Christian Old Testament manuscripts also have advanced the view that there existed from pre-Christian days illustrated Jewish Bible manuscripts, presumably in Greek and from the diaspora. As Christian art developed, it seems to have taken over this Jewish iconographic and illustrative tradition. Most of early Christian art has, alas, perished, as also has Jewish art of this ancient era. Yet the traditions of that art were taken over into Byzantine and European Christian art as it developed, and thence, of course, into modern cultural traditions.

The Jewish tradition itself seems to have adapted much of its illustrative technique and some of the scenes it portrayed from pagan Greek illustration of classical works. It might be added that these Jewish manuscripts were probably not of the whole Bible. Copies of the whole Bible could not be made before the codex, that is, the manuscript in the form of a book, came into wide use. Previously the manuscript copies of books had been written on rolls or scrolls, as were the Dead Sea manuscripts.

Thus we find a variety of Jewish attitudes towards the illustration and representation of figures, and particularly towards the illumination of biblical manuscripts. This serves, firstly, to show us another source and type of resource that should be consulted in the study of ancient Judaism. Secondly, it shows how varied were the attitudes towards the third commandment. It raises interesting questions as to the relationship of Palestinian and diaspora Jewries, and also graphically illuminates aspects of the cultural relationship between Judaism and pagan Hellenistic culture.

This relationship must have been extremely complex. This has already been seen in the variety of types of Jewish composition in Greek. There is, in addition, a variety of evidence recently assembled and reassessed on the relationship between these two cultures in the land of Israel itself. It seems clear that the traditional delineation of a pious, Semitic-speaking Palestinian Judaism set against a rather independent, more liberal Greek-speaking diaspora, must be set aside.

For the extent of Greek culture in the land of Israel itself was considerable. The Greek manuscripts among the Dead Sea Scrolls have already been mentioned, and these included copies of the Greek Scriptures. In addition, a very important Greek Scriptural manuscript was found in the caves south of Qumrân, which contain deposits from the period of the

Bar Kochba revolt (c. 132 C.E.). Numerous inscriptions have been found in Jerusalem and its environs dating from the last-pre-Christian centuries down to the destruction of the second Temple. About a fifth of these inscriptions are Greek and the rest Hebrew and Aramaic. The personal names used in Palestine also witness to this penetration of some elements of Greek culture; the name of Antigonos of Socho, the noted early rabbi, is an example, and is far from the only one.

Beyond all of this, the courts of the royal houses, both Maccabean and Herodian, were deeply Hellenized. Herod, in particular, ran a Greek oriental court, including the assembling of men of letters and philosophy around him. The most famous of these was the Syrian, Nicholas of Damascus, whose multi-volumed history served as one of Josephus' chief sources. Nicholas also acted as Herod's envoy on a number of delicate international missions. Herod's building of the Greek city of Caesaria Maritima as his capital was another act in this direction. Yet, Herod was quite careful to keep the pagan religious elements of this court life out of the areas of Jerusalem and Judah proper, where they might have caused great strife, as did the banners of the Roman legions not so long after-wards.

Furthermore, it should be remembered that throughout the land of Israel there were Greek cities and settlements, as well as settlements of Hellenized Phoenicians and so forth. Indeed, in the north the famous Decapolis was a group of ten cities which produced a number of important pagan writers and thinkers during this period. A settlement of Hellenized Phoenicians is known to have lived at Marisa at the foot of the Judean Hills, not far from Beth Shemesh. These were not isolated cases. The relations between the Jews and these various groups of settlers were not consistently good and, indeed, there was at some periods considerable enmity be-tween them. Yet the possible influence of such groups as these in forming the intellectual and spiritual atmosphere in the country should not be underestimated.

In addition to the above, various studies have shown a

greater or lesser measure of Greek influence in the early rabbinic sources. One series of studies has investigated the possible influence of Hellenistic story types on rabbinic tales about revered teachers. Others have sought explicitly Greek elements mentioned by the rabbinic sources, even finding certain of the rabbinic methods of exegesis to be related to Alexandrian exegesis of Homer.

The cumulative result of all these studies has been to raise quite acutely the question of the influence of Hellenism among the Jews in Graeco-Roman Palestine. Such an influence can no longer be discounted; on the other hand, no solid evidence has emerged for a degree of Hellenization like that which apparently took place in the diaspora. Evidence for a meeting between Judaism and the intellectual culture of Hellenism within the land of Israel has not yet emerged, although it is a possibility that must still be left open. What is clear is that there was a penetration of Greek language and elements of Greek culture which was really quite considerable.

It is well to bear this situation in mind when attempting to assess the relationships between the Jewish community in the land of Israel and the communities of the diaspora. Obviously, not all the diaspora communities could have had the same relationships with Jerusalem, and for many of them our information is minimal. Nonetheless, there is a good deal of information indicating that the relationships were quite intimate. A number of diaspora communities had synagogues or other centres in Jerusalem at this time. Moreover, the institution of pilgrimage brought large numbers of Jews from the diaspora, as well as from the further reaches of the land of Israel, to Jerusalem on the occasion of the major Jewish pilgrimage festivals. After all, Jerusalem held pride of place in the Jewish world. The distances from Asia Minor or Egypt were not very great, nor was Syria excessively far off.

The problem of the relationship between the Palestinian and Alexandrian communities has been particularly discussed in connection with the authority for establishment of the canon of scripture. The difficulty is that in the Christian Old Testament in Greek there are included a number of works which do not occur in the Hebrew Bible. These additional books, called the Apocrypha, are uniformly Jewish in origin. Some of them were written in Hebrew and translated into Greek, while others were composed in Greek.

Now the Greek translation of the Bible was of Jewish provenance, but we do not have any copies of it made by Jews, except for a few fragments. All the copies which we have are Christian, and the oldest of these date from the third or fourth centuries of this era. In them the additional books appear, and they are also listed in Christian lists of biblical books from the same period. Since Christian authority for scripture derived from Jewish usage, some scholars have hypothesized that there was a different canon, that is a different authoritative collection of scripture, in Alexandria than in Palestine and, for that reason, the Christians who accepted the Alexandrian usage had a wider collection.

There are a number of rather compelling reasons for rejecting this construct. These include the following. Firstly, there does not in fact seem to have been a firmly established Christian usage. The books included and excluded by the various early Christian authorities show a measure of variation which would have been impossible had there been a firmly established collection that the Church received. Secondly, in addition to the difference in number of books, the collections from Christian and Jewish sources are distinguished by the different order of the books. In the Hebrew Bible the books are arranged in three parts which seem to reflect, incidentally, natural stages in the growth of the collection. These are the Torah or the Pentateuch, the Prophets (containing also Joshua, Judges, Samuel and Kings, and not including Daniel) and the Writings, all the other books. In the Greek Old Testament the Torah is intact, but all the other books are arranged by literary types and historical order, not by the growth of the collections. Yet, there are a number of Jewish Greek sources which seem familiar with the tripartite division of the Hebrew Bible. This would imply that the distinctive order of the Christian Old Testament is perhaps not of Jewish origin.

In fact, there is evidence from the land of Israel that the third of the parts of the Hebrew Bible was only just coming to take on its final form in the period which we are discussing. The Christian usage probably separated from Jewish usage before the collection had finally crystallized and before it came to be regarded with the same measure of sanctity as the Torah and the Prophets in the eyes of the community. This being the case, it is possible that the variation of Christian usage was a reflection of variation of Jewish usage and pre-served a maximal collection, while the Jewish Hebrew sources preserved a minimal one.

It should be stressed that the above suggestion is supported by a good deal of technical argumentation which is best left for treatment elsewhere. What is important about it is that it seems to do away finally with the "Alexandrian Canon Hypothesis". This means that it is no longer necessary to assume that Alexandrian Jewry saw sufficient authority in-vested in itself to establish a collection of sacred Scripture which was different from that established and accepted by the authorities in the land of Israel. Instead, the new suggestion takes account of the complexity of the evidence both on the Hebrew and on the Greek side, and provides a way of account-ing for it in terms which accord with the other things known about the relationship between the various communities.

Thus, the relationship between Judaism and Hellenism seems to have been a rather complex one. There are many unknowns and in a number of matters the two cultures seem to have conflicted. Yet there were also levels at which there was integration between them and attempts to explain the one to the other. Two final comments should perhaps be made.

The first is that, although Jewish authors and thinkers made considerable attempts to explain Judaism in terms which Greeks could understand, their anti-idolatrous polemic re-mained as strong as ever. Although paganism has taken on quite highly developed forms of religious philosophy, develop-

ing a monism that in many ways approached Jewish monotheism, no attempt was made by the Jews either to understand
or combat this sort of religion. Jewish polemic centred upon
those aspects of paganism which had traditionally been
attacked by Jews, from ancient times—the absurdity of
worship of images (with which many Hellenistic pagans
would have agreed), immorality of paganism and so forth.
Judaism in these matters was very much on the offensive,
although it may be questioned at what sort of audience this
anti-idolatrous polemic was directed—perhaps a Jewish one.
There were certain Jewish propaganda works clearly intended
for the pagan world, such as the *Sibylline Oracles*. These were
Jewish (and later Christian) oracles, attributed to the famed
sibyl in whose name numerous oracles were fabricated in that
period. These works are first and foremost a glorification of
Judaism and prediction of victory and success of the Jewish
people.

A final feature that must be recalled in assessing Jewish-
Gentile relationships in the Hellenistic world is that Judaism
was an actively proselytizing religion in this era. There is
ample evidence of this, gained from the attitudes to proselytes in writings as old as the Book of Judith, as well as from
references in Greek and Roman sources. The spread of Judaism is to be seen partly in the context of the spread of
oriental religions of other sorts in the Graeco-Roman world,
a well-known development. It seems to have had particular
currency among women, men perhaps being inhibited because of the requirement of circumcision; and even larger
than the number of true proselytes was the number of the "god-
fearing", of those who accepted a measure of Jewish custom
and belief without taking the final step of proselytization. It
is, of course, in this context that much of the spread of early
Christianity must be understood, and that some of Paul's
conflicts with the Jerusalem community of early Christianity
must be interpreted.

10

GNOSTICISM AND JUDAISM

Recent times have seen the publication of the English translation of the Gnostic manuscripts in Coptic from Nag Hammadi in Egypt. The general character of this find was discussed in Chapter 1, and in the present chapter we shall attempt to make some preliminary comments on the relationship between Gnosticism and Judaism, without claiming to exhaust this topic. The Gnostic texts are often extremely difficult to interpret and to set in their social and religious context.

The Gnostics were members of a group of religious sects which lived in the Roman and early Christian periods. Gnosticism posed a major challenge to orthodox Christianity in the second and third centuries of this era. It was a diffuse and complex religious movement, finding expression in Christian, pagan and, apparently, in Jewish forms. Until the discovery of the Nag Hammadi manuscripts, our knowledge of Gnosticism was derived primarily from the writings of its Christian opponents.

In some ways Gnosticism is a very understandable growth from the general spirit of Hellenistic religiosity which we have already described. Its chief thrust was an attempt to provide salvation. People had to be saved from the entrapment in this world of matter which was quite alien. The force of Gnosticism is the revelation of certain sorts of knowledge (*gnōsis*) about man and his condition, which knowledge enables him to grasp and hold.

The *Fourth Book of Ezra*, not a Gnostic composition by any means, was written about the end of the first century C.E. It is an apocalypse, characterized by a good deal of theological heart-searching. In the course of his agonizing, the author of the *Fourth Book of Ezra* develops an idea of "original sin" from which some sort of redemption was needed. The author, writing in the aftermath of the destruction of the Temple by Titus in the year 70 C.E., is much concerned how this should have come about. Man was flawed, he concludes, from his creation. He cries at one point, "O you, Adam, what have you done? for though it was you who sinned, the fall was not yours alone, but ours who are your descendants". Elsewhere he summons God before the bar of His own justice and reproaches him for creating man with the ability to sin and yet punishing him for sin. Ultimately, it was that sin that led to the destruction. Paul faces a similar issue in his view of sin, although it is not formulated as a result of the destruction of the Temple. His resolution of the dilemma thus raised is in Christology; the author of the *Fourth Book of Ezra* finds his in the promised vindication of the righteous at the end of days. The two solutions resemble one another in the way they respond to the problem: both see the resolution as coming from outside. An outside intervention or force will resolve the conflict.

The Gnostics were also faced by issues of the alienation of man in this world. For them man is completely alienated from this world and from his own body. The true man is different from this world, utterly other than it. He does not come from the world in any way, and the whole of the cosmos is demonic. The problem is man's imprisonment in this world. Man contains a spark of the divine which is the pure part of him. This spark can be released and reunited with the Godhead of which it is a part through the saving knowledge or *gnōsis*. The Godhead is utterly apart from, other than and unknowable by anyone in this world.

Most of the Gnostic systems are provided with a myth of

cosmogony which explains how this spark of the divine came to be entrapped by matter. They are often also furnished with a myth of redemption in which the Godhead, by some sort of intervention in the material world, makes known to the Gnostic the fact of his true alienness. These myths sometimes make use of Jewish and Christian language and imagery, but always in a very particular and tendentious way. Since the created world is demonic, the God who created it is a demon and so, in Gnostic interpretations of Judaism and Christianity, the God of Creation, called the Demiurge, is identified with the God of the Old Testament and regarded as a demonic figure. For this reason, scholars maintained for years that Gnosticism should be regarded as originating in a pagan-Christian mix and not from Jewish sources.

With the renewed interest in Gnosticism engendered by the availability of the Nag Hammadi treatises, the question of the possible Jewish origins of some sorts of Gnosticism has been re-opened. It seems that certain of the Nag Hammadi documents and fragments should be regarded as reflecting a Jewish gnosticism. A striking example is a text entitled the *Testimony of Truth*. In this document, which on the whole is clearly Christian, are embedded older fragments. Some of these are even marked off in the manuscript by short horizontal lines in the margin of the codex. Certain of them have points of contact with orthodox Jewish interpretations of scripture, even though the theological stance they take is completely Gnostic.

Much of Gnostic writing utilizing the Bible concentrates on the Creation stories in the *Book of Genesis*. In a fragment in the *Testimony of Truth*, Eve's seduction by the serpent is related, and how she ate the forbidden fruit. In the Gnostic world-view this world and its creator were evil. So the values of the biblical story were reversed, the serpent is a good being, Eve's teacher and the wisest of all animals. His "seduction" of Eve was in fact his revelation of true knowledge to her. Eve gave Adam the fruit to eat, that is, she communicated this revealed wisdom to him. This stance is clearly Gnostic, and behind the exegesis lies a word-play in Aramaic in which the words for "Eve", "serpent", "beast" and "reveal" are very similar. Parenthetically, it may be remarked that this is not the only case in which an Aramaic expression has been found to underlie Gnostic terminology.

In this passage the actual Gnostic views expressed are rather simple, and it lacks any Christian elements. It contains features of the exegesis of Genesis which can be paralleled in orthodox Jewish sources and, most remarkable, its literary style is that of rabbinic Midrash. It is the opinion of its editor that this particular fragment is a piece of old, Jewish, Gnostic material, preserved in the Christian, Gnostic *Testimony of Truth*.

A different sort of Jewish background is demanded when the extensive traditions associated with Seth in Gnostic texts are examined. At one level, many scholars are of the view that the document called the *Apocalypse of Adam* from Codex V is a Jewish, not a Christian, Gnostic piece. Be this as it may, what is clear is that the figure of Seth, relatively little developed in the Apocrypha and surviving Pseudepigrapha, takes on a major role as a revealer figure and first true Gnostic in a series of Gnostic documents. Already, from the heresiologists, the Christian opponents of Gnosticism, it was known that there were Gnostic groups whom they called "Sethians", for whom he played a particularly central role.

An examination of traditions associated with Seth in a number of Jewish and Christian sources reveals that this figure has undergone extensive development in these varying traditions. It has been argued that it is hard to see all of this as independent growth, and that behind the Gnostic Seth traditions must lie a Jewish development of the figure of Seth, which is not witnessed to by any of our surviving sources.

Another argument has been developed from the examination of the figure of Sophia (Greek for "wisdom") in Valentinian Gnosticism. A careful comparison has been carried out of Sophia in Valentinian teaching with the figure of personified Wisdom which appears in the biblical and apocryphal wisdom books. This comparison seems to show that Jewish speculations on the nature of Wisdom (which themselves, it may be added, might well have a mythological background) provided the characteristics which were taken over by Valentinian Sophia and developed in line with Gnostic views.

Again, the body of Greek Gnostic or Gnosticizing material called the *Corpus Hermeticum*, has been known for long centuries. Supposedly a revelation to Hermes Trismegistus (Thrice-Great), who is the Egyptian god Thoth syncretized with Greek Hermes, these documents provide a fascinating insight into pagan Gnosticism of the early Christian centuries. They are much influenced by middle Platonism, as is a great deal of Gnostic writing. The first of the treatises which make up this body of writings is called the *Poimandres*. It relates a creation myth and in it Jewish influence has been detected, particularly of the creation story in *Genesis*. No Christian features have been found.

Thus, in the present state of learning it seems impossible to answer the question whether Gnosticism is a growth out of Judaism. It does not seem likely that there can ever be a single unambiguous answer to the question of Gnostic origins. That there was a Jewish form of Gnosticism seems very likely now, and perhaps the evidence from rabbinic texts about dualistic Jewish heretics should be re-examined in this context. That itself is a major innovation for the study of Judaism, for it is likely that this Jewish Gnosticism has roots going back into the pre-Christian era. Moreover, it also seems to be probable that from the further careful study of the newly published Coptic Gnostic manuscripts a good deal of further information on this topic will emerge.

There is a certain similarity between some of the Gnostic descriptions of the celestial world and some of those in the Jewish "Chariot" mystical books. Even more like Gnostic views is, strangely, the Lurianic Kabbalah, or mystical doctrine, that developed in Safed in the Galilee in the time following the expulsion of the Jews from Spain in the year 1492. Nonetheless, the question can be raised as to how far the sorts of speculations embodied in *earlier* Jewish mystical writings may have influenced the development of Gnosticism.

Scholem clearly showed that the Jewish mystical tradition, including ascent to the environs of the Godhead for purposes of gaining theosophical knowledge, is much more ancient than was suspected. If his arguments are accepted, this activity was going on in the early second century C.E. and most likely before that. In Chapter 4 we have discussed the connection of the terminological traditions found in the earlier Jewish writings with those of the mystical books. Scholem's studies have been important since they illuminated an aspect of Jewish religious life in the first centuries of this era which had previously been ignored, or at least played down.

The mystical approach necessarily was concerned with techniques of ascent through the heavens, the description of the celestial world and particularly of the environs of the deity. It seems to have developed out of certain types of religious experience documented in Jewish literature of the period of the Second Temple. The concern with ascent and the description of the heavens or spheres and their perils and the like are also to be found in certain Gnostic texts. The ecstatic description of God enthroned also seems to have some parallels in Gnostic materials. Yet it is also plain that, to date, no clear connections have been shown to exist between these two traditions.

Many questions thus surround the Jewish sources of Gnosticism, on which further development in studies of the corpus of new texts may cast light. Clear conclusions cannot yet be drawn, therefore, as to where and which types of Judaism contributed to the formation of Gnosticism. That there were such contributions, however, now seems beyond doubt.

It is also unclear whether it can be assumed that there was Jewish mystical activity properly speaking before the second century C.E. at the very earliest. Heavenly ascents and descriptions of the heavenly realm are to be found in the literature, and it is reasonable to assume that these reflect some actual ecstatic practice going on in the society. Still, it is not clear that this activity was mystical in its purposes and

functions, and this is not indicated by the evidence that we
have in the sources at present available.

11

UNEXPLORED LEGACIES OF JUDAISM

THE CHALLENGES

The study of Judaism in the period in which Christianity arose and rabbinic Judaism began to evolve its characteristic forms is crucial to understanding the past and present of western culture. Unexpected and exciting aspects of Judaism from the third century B.C.E. to the first century C.E. have already been illuminated by the uncovering of new sources. For the future, two great challenges lie ahead. The first is the careful, diligent search for even more knowledge about the past, above all the attempt to make available as many new sources and as much new information as possible. The other task is even more demanding. It is the study of the new sources and the integration of what they teach us into the picture we draw of the past. That picture of the past is of central importance for the understanding of our present.

Many exciting discoveries lie ahead in the quest after new sources. Numerous Dead Sea Scrolls still await publication. Although most of the large scrolls have now been made public, hundreds of documents are still in the hands of their editors. The impact of the manuscripts of the *Book of Enoch* illustrates how revolutionary such publications can be. There are documents from other finds in the Judean desert which are still in the hands of their editors. The Dāliyeh papyri on the one hand and the Bar Kochba papers on the other are likely to contribute much, particularly to historians and linguists. There are vast amounts of papyrus material scattered around museums and universities which could contain treasures. Much material from the Cairo Geniza is still untapped, particularly texts in the collection in the Soviet Union. It does not need to be said that the quicker material is published the better. Here the editors of the Nag Hammadi codices made an excellent start by publishing first translations and a facsimile edition, so that all scholars can get quick access to the texts.

Less romantic than the search after manuscript fragments in caves in the Judean desert is the careful study of the whole of the manuscript tradition of texts which are already known. Here it should be stressed that the very foundation of the historian's work must be reliable texts of his source documents. Many of the writings of the period we are discussing are known only in very poor editions, prepared a century or so ago, when interest in these matters was quite lively. Some progress is being made in this direction, and new editions of a number of works have appeared in recent years. There is still a great deal to do.

There are some works of Philo, for example, that perished in Greek, and only survived in Armenian translations made from the Greek. Most of these have never been translated into English. Those that have were translated from a text prepared in the eighteenth century. Clearly new editions and English translations are urgently needed, and such are under way. There are, furthermore, some works connected with the Philonic writings in Armenian, but which are from another hand. These are very important since they constitute the only non-Philonic writings of this type to have survived. Yet these have been around and known for 200 years without an English translation being made. Philo is not the only case. Only now has a new edition of the Ethiopic text of the *Book of Enoch* appeared which will replace that published at the end of the last century from the manuscripts then in Europe. Searches for new manuscripts in Ethiopia are likely to turn up even more rich material. No new edition of the *Book of Jubilees* has been published for many decades.

In addition to the need for new editions of works which are

already known, a search for new texts is imperative. This search should be made in known libraries and in unstudied manuscript traditions and collections. Not long ago a major new Aramaic translation of the Bible was discovered in the Vatican Library in a manuscript with the wrong title stamped on the spine. The manuscript traditions of many oriental churches have scarcely been explored. Many of the collections of manuscripts have not been catalogued, or else the catalogues are not readily accessible. Only less than half of the existing Armenian manuscripts have been catalogued in detail, and there are thousands that have never been catalogued at all. For seventy years or so, no serious study has been devoted to the subject of Jewish literature of the period of the Second Temple preserved in church Slavonic, except for the work of one or two scholars in recent years. The situation in Georgian is quite unknown, except for a volume of editions of the Apocrypha published recently by the Georgian Academy of Sciences.

These languages doubtless sound very obscure, as indeed they are. Still, the riches discovered in the Ethiopic tradition or the situation with the Armenian Philo or the fact that the *Book of the Secrets of Enoch* and the *Apocalypse of Abraham* are found only in Old Church Slavonic should alert us to the fact that these traditions may well preserve material which has not turned up in Greek and Latin. Even the study of these latter sources could well be intensified. In particular, the study of the hagiographic traditions, the stories which clustered around revered men of the past, may prove very fruitful for the study of Judaism and also of early Christianity.

In the preceding pages, little mention has been made of one of the areas in which scholarly interest is now awakening, namely, the way in which these Jewish works were transmitted, used and re-worked by the various Christian churches. There is a large body of literature dealing with biblical figures and subjects that is partly created and partly transmitted by the various Christian churches. Certain of these books have been found to be indubitably Jewish writings, for instance the

Apocrypha and the generally recognized Pseudepigrapha. Others are under greater debate, while still others are clearly Christian reworkings of writings based on Jewish traditional material, oral or written.

The study of this kind of literature should commence from an examination of its use in the Christian churches that transmitted it, for only then can a sensitivity be developed which will enable us to evaluate it as material related to the history of Judaism. For a study of this sort, cooperation is needed between those involved in working on the older Jewish texts, and those with expertise in Christian literature and mediaeval literature in general. Many of these traditions had wide circulation, and not only in the East, but through the various European languages and cultures as well. Much may well be learned by careful examination of the rich body of Irish apocryphal literature or of popular traditions in old French.

A good deal also remains to be done in the study of mediaeval Jewish manuscripts in search of these texts. Above we have noted that a fragment of the *Book of Jubilees* was included in the introduction to a mediaeval Jewish medical book. If Syriac is put into Hebrew letters it can be read by an educated Jew as Aramaic. This happened to the *Wisdom of Solomon*, which was known in its Syriac version, in Hebrew characters, in mediaeval Spain. At the same time, we also know of the translation into Hebrew in the Middle Ages of large portions of the *Biblical Antiquities* of Pseudo-Philo and this translation was made out of the Latin. This is not an isolated instance. The same seems to have been true of some parts of a work entitled *The Lives of the Prophets*, and of other pieces of Jewish literature that have survived only in Christian languages.

Just as it is necessary to investigate the way these documents and traditions were transmitted in the Christian churches, so questions must be asked about their Jewish transmission. First, lines of contact between cultures can perhaps be traced by examining the sources of borrowing. Second, perhaps some measure of direct Jewish transmission from antiquity may be discovered. It is by no means evident, for example, that the *Book of Jubilees* fragments mentioned were translated back into Hebrew from another language. Or, to take another example, a mediaeval Jewish legend called the *Midrash of Shemhazai and Azazel* provides an intermediate link between ancient Jewish Noah traditions, some Seth traditions preserved in Armenian, and some Gnostic Sethian traditions. So, clearly, the mediaeval Jewish tradition should be examined scrupulously for its contribution to this material.

One final important source of material remains, if the possibility of new archaeological discovery is discounted for the purposes of our present discussion. This is a careful study of the numerous quotations from apocryphal literature to be found particularly in Christian writers of the first millennium. The names of many lost Pseudepigrapha are known from lists compiled by ancient authorities for various purposes. Fragments of many of these lost writings can be recovered by a careful combing of patristic writings, Byzantine chronicles and other mediaeval works which used and cited books now lost. Mention was made in an earlier chapter of the old, pioneering collection by J. Fabricius, made in the eighteenth century. In 1920, the learned Englishman, M. R. James, published a collection of material with which he was familiar which belonged to these books. His learning is hard to rival. Yet a careful examination of the traditions of the oriental churches, and also of material which is not presented as citations but as narrative in Greek and Latin, might well prove fruitful. Preliminary work in this direction has shown that sometimes the shape and even the character of these lost works can be recovered, occasionally with the help of papyrus or manuscript discoveries, from Qumrân and elsewhere.

Finally, many of these traditions have a life of their own and a development in the Moslem tradition. This is often illuminating and occasionally very important for location and definition of certain problems. It still has to be systematically researched from the viewpoint of Jewish literary history. It is not difficult to catalogue the different types of Jewish religious expression that existed. The names of sects are known, books have survived, archaeology has made its contribution, Jewish and Christian traditions have made their statements. The unresolved issues are precisely those of the broader picture. How did these various forms of Judaism relate to one another, if at all? What was the sort of religious outlook of a given individual? What was the complexion of Judaism in a given area or at a specific time?

Here one of the chief features of the religious life of the period of the Second Temple seems to come to the fore. It was a period of great variety of religious expression. This was true of the religions of the Graeco-Roman world in general and of Judaism in particular. Josephus speaks of four philosophies—Pharisees, Sadducees, Essenes and Zealots. There were very many forms of religious thinking if the evidence of the Apocrypha and Pseudepigrapha is taken into account. How rigid were Josephus' "philosophies"? What variety of ideas could they tolerate without expulsion of their advocates? Which of the Apocrypha and Pseudepigrapha, if any, can be attributed to what group? How did the different groups regard one another?

In this complex of issues is hidden the key to a judicious presentation of the "balance of power" among ideas within Judaism during the period of the Second Temple. Moreover, that "balance of power" which would be illuminated by answering the above questions would bear mostly on the situation in the land of Israel. Relations between Palestinian Jewry and that of the Diaspora, as well as the multi-faceted variety of Diaspora Jewry itself, raise a further new series of issues.

In very broadest terms, it seems that a rejection of idolatry and an adherence to the Torah of Moses and the Temple in Jerusalem must have been common to all Jews in that age. Those whose practice differed radically from that of the whole community, such as the acceptance of a variant calendar or the rejection of the validity of the Temple and its priesthood, probably put themselves outside the community of Israel and became a sect. Such were the Qumrân covenanters. How did those who accepted the common institutions regard one another, at points where their interpretations differed? Such differences clearly existed between the Pharisees and the Sadducees, yet they seem to have shared the common institutions and perhaps differed little more from one another than did a Hellenized but faithful Jew like Philo from both of them. Here we approach the question of normativism. Was there a normative Judaism, a generally accepted form from which the other forms of Judaism were seen as diverging?

Josephus is at great pains to present the Pharisees as the dominant group, followed by most of the people. This is a picture that is corroborated, it seems, by the Nahum Commentary from Qumrân. Does this mean that Pharisaism was normative? Semantic word-chopping, one might respond; perhaps so, but important nonetheless to determine. Pharisaism seems to have been dominant in Palestine, especially towards the end of the period under discussion. But did the broad public support that the Pharisaic teachers apparently enjoyed mean that the Sadducees were considered to be in some measure illegitimate or unacceptable? This does not seem to be indicated by our sources, although a situation was to arise soon after the Destruction in 70 C.E. when this would come to be the case.

Certain assumptions concerning the composition of the religious and intellectual traditions of Judaism at this time have been placed under scrutiny. The place of the speculative tradition, the role of ascent activity, the existence of the sorts of Judaism which fed into Gnosticism, all these and more come to enrich the picture that is gained simply by consulting Josephus, the New Testament and rabbinic literature. How does this sort of material cohere with the divisions of Pharisees and Sadducees we know from Josephus?

What seems to be becoming clear is that the simple line of development of apocalyptic literature along the eschatological axis, from the prophets to the apocalypses, from the apocalypses to Jesus, must be reassessed. In fact, this eschatological development seems to have been one of the most prominent features of Jewish thought at that time, and Jesus seems to have been related to it. Yet, the phenomenon of the Jewish apocalypses is very much more complex, and indeed it may well be asked whether any actual group or body of literature fosters the eschatological dimension to the exclusion of all others. That is an unreal view, as is shown by the mixture of eschatology and *halacha* (Jewish law) at Qumrân and the mixture of eschatology, pseudo-science and speculation in the literary apocalypses.

Indeed, the phenomena of the apocalypses serve well to illustrate the difficulties we now encounter. It would be simplest, of course, if all the apocalypses came from the same sect or trend in society. The least we might hope for would be to have some evidence as to which of the groups known to us produced apocalypses. But this we do not have either. What can be stated is that this literary form was apparently remarkably widespread. It seems to have had a chronological range from at least the third century B.C.E. until the end of the period we are discussing. There are apocalypses of various religious colourings, from the clearly sectarian to some which are perhaps from circles close to the Pharisees. There are apocalypses which were written in Aramaic, in Hebrew and, apparently, in Greek. How are the interests and types which are found in the apocalypses to be related to the various groups and trends which are known to have existed in society?

Together with the sort of problem which the apocalypses raise, there is another which impedes our understanding. This is the question of the relationship between Judaism and Hellenism and the form it took, both in the land of Israel and in the Diaspora. This problem is not an easy one, and we have seen in Chapter 9 that it is necessary to reckon with a whole range of relationships, both within the land of Israel and outside it. How deeply did Hellenism penetrate into those types of Judaism which continued to have influence in succeeding generations? How far did the varieties of this relationship provide early patterns which Judaism of later times followed in its relationship with the cultures of the surrounding peoples?

From this range of problems and this approach it should be possible to achieve a different perspective on the place that earliest Christianity held within the range of Jewish religious expression. Clearly, the picture of Judaism looks very different when it is drawn from as many sources as possible, and when it is drawn merely from the perspective of Christianity, or that of rabbinic Judaism for that matter. The Christian sources form a valuable body of evidence about Judaism in the first century. The question is how far the interests of Christianity reflect a central type of Judaism, insofar as such a central type existed. For example, it seems to be very important for understanding the place of Christianity in Judaism to realise that a whole range of speculative interests is missing from the New Testament. That realization is more significant when the role of these interests in Judaism is understood and properly evaluated, not played down. Then the particular aspect of Christianity becomes more striking than ever.

The ramifications of this methodological approach are rather far-reaching. The primary focus of the historian of Judaism should be to present as balanced and true a picture of what was going on as he can. *Later* configurations of Judaism and Christianity may have only a peripheral importance in determining the actual situation that existed. Yet it is from the description of that situation that most is to be learned for our own times.

Another important aspect of this renewed examination is the recovery of what was going on in the third and perhaps the fourth century B.C.E. Since we lack any sources outside the Bible, it is important to try to penetrate back beyond the literature that has survived. It has been an open question whether the surviving Apocrypha and Pseudepigrapha contain later forms of more ancient traditions. If this is the case, then they might be used, albeit with great caution, to throw some light on Judaism of the time of the First Temple. The recovery of an intellectual tradition of a scientific nature with Babylonian affinities certainly opens up new vistas into ancient Judaism.

For all of these concerns in the history of Judaism and Christianity it is imperative to realise how important is the study of all the phenomena of Judaism in the period of the Second Temple. It is also important because this was an age of transition from older forms of religious belief and types of religion to those which were to become dominant for the following millennia. In Judaism there was a transition from sacred tradition to sacred book. The role of the Torah and gradually of the other parts of Scripture became pre-eminent. Gradually the forms of religious writing changed, reflecting the developing attitudes to sacred Scripture. This was the last period for many centuries in which a major part of Jewish religious literature was written neither as commentary or as extended commentary on Scripture.

This was also an age in which a consolidation of the actual textual tradition of the biblical books happened. There was a movement from the variety of textual types which are documented, for example, at Qumrân, to the single, proto-Massoretic type dominant at Muraba'at and in rabbinic and later Judaism. As well as transition in attitudes to scripture and its text, this age was also one in which the institutions were formed that facilitated the enormous change in the forms of Judaism which the destruction of the Temple brought about. There was a shift from the uniquely Temple-centred institutions of an earlier age towards the synagogue and academy which became the central features of later Judaism.

Thus, one important dimension of the age here studied is that it helps us to understand how Judaism came to take on its later forms. By the same token, dimensions of Jewish religious expression may be recaptured which did not survive the destruction of the Temple. Since this was the last age before the present in which Jews lived in their own political State, with Judaism as the dominant culture, insight into the types of Judaism in that earlier State may prove of considerable interest for students of the present scene of Jewish religious creativity. The relationship between varied forms of Jewish religious expression in a Jewish society is a great concern today. Diversity in the relationship between Judaism of the Diaspora and that of the land of Israel is a problem with a familiar ring. The self-understanding of a Hebrew-speaking Christian minority in a majority Jewish culture is an "old-new" challenge.

The same sort of parallel, with admitted differences, can be drawn between the variety of relationships between Judaism and Hellenism and between Judaism and western culture today. The problems are similar and, in many ways, like resolutions of the tensions between the two have been sought. Continued study may uncover a more general phenomenology of that relationship. In any case, the implications of the historical study can scarcely be ignored by those concerned with the ongoing stream of Jewish, Christian and Greek thought in the West.

Bibliography

The Bibliography includes the chief sources for further reading on subjects dealt with in this book. With one or two exceptions, works in foreign languages have been excluded. Certain of the books and articles listed are of a particularly technical character, and these are marked with an asterisk. The Bibliography has been divided into sections by subject, with bibliographical and general works preceding those devoted to specific topics. It should be borne in mind that certain specific topics are dealt with extensively in the books included in the "General Works" category. Only translations of primary sources are included, but references to the published editions of Greek, Latin or Semitic texts are included in them.

1. BIBLIOGRAPHIES

Burchard, Ch., *Bibliographie zu den Handschriften von Toten Meer*, *ZAW Beiheft* 76, 89, Berlin: Töpelmann, 1959, 1965. This bibliography is supplemented regularly in the journal *Revue de Qumrân*.

Charlesworth, J. H., *The Pseudepigrapha and Modern Research*,

Septuagint and Cognate Studies 7, Missoula: Scholars Press, 1976.

Delling, G., *Bibliographie zur jüdisch-hellenistischen und inter-testamentarischen Literatur, Texte und Untersuchungen* 106.2, Berlin: Akademie, 1975.

Fitzmyer, J. A., *The Dead Sea Scrolls, Major Publications and Tools for Study*, Sources for Biblical Study 8, Missoula, Scholars Press, 1977.

Scholar, D., *Nag Hammadi Bibliography*, Nag Hammadi Studies 1, Leiden; Brill, 1971. This bibliography is supplemented regularly in the journal *Novum Testamentum*.

In addition to the above, the book by M. Hengel (below, section 2) is provided with particularly rich bibliographical details. A detailed and analytical annual bibliography relating to this field is the *Elenchus Bibliographicus* published in conjunction with the journal *Biblica*. Useful summaries of current work may also be found in the periodicals *New Testament Abstracts* and *Old Testament Abstracts*.

2. GENERAL WORKS

de Jonge M. and Safrai S. (eds.), *Compendia Rerum Iudaicarum ad Novum Testamentum*, Vols. 1–2, Assen: van Gorcum, 1974–76. These first two volumes of a projected multi-volume work deal with the political, social and economic history of the Jews in the first century. They are in English.

Hengel, M., *Judaism and Hellenism*, 2 Vols., London: SCM, 1973.

Schürer, E., *History of the Jewish People at the Time of Christ*, (ed. and rev. by G. Vermès and F. Millar), Vol. 1, Edinburgh: T. & T. Clark, 1973. This is the first volume of a revision and updating of this classic work. Two more volumes are to follow.

Useful articles may also be found in *Encyclopaedia Judaica*, 16 vols., Jerusalem: Keter, 1971–72, in *The Interpreters Dictionary of the Bible*, 4 Vols., Nashville: Abingdon, 1962; and in the *Supplementary Volume* to that work, Nashville: Abingdon, 1976.

3. PRIMARY SOURCES

Apocrypha and Pseudepigrapha.
Charles, R. H., *The Apocrypha and Pseudepigrapha of the Old Testament*, 2 Vols., Oxford: 1913 (hereafter cited as "Charles, *Apot*").

James, M. R., *The Lost Apocrypha of the Old Testament*, London: S.P.C.K., 1920.

Coptic Gnostic Codices:
Robinson, J. M. (ed.), *The Nag Hammadi Library*, New York: Doubleday, 1977.

Dead Sea Scrolls:
There are various translations, such as those by G. Vermès (Harmonsworth: Penguin, 1965); A. Dupont-Sommer (tr. G. Vermès) (Oxford: Blackwells, 1961); T. Gaster (New York: Doubleday, 1977).

Elephantini Papyri:

Cowley, A., *Aramaic Papyri of the Fifth Century*, 1923; repr. Onasbrück: Zeller, 1967.

Porten, B., *The Archives from Elephantini; the Life of an Ancient Jewish Military Colony*, Berkeley: Univ. of California, 1968.

Josephus:

Marcus R. and Feldman L., *Josephus*, 9 Vols., Loeb Classical Library, London & Cambridge, Mass.: Heinemann & Harvard, 1926–1965.

New Testament Apocrypha:

Hennecke, E. and Schneemelcher, W., *The New Testament Apocrypha*, ed. R. McL. Wilson, Philadelphia: Westminster, 1963–66.

James, M. R., *The Apocryphal New Testament*, Cambridge, 1923.

Philo:

Colson, F. H. and G. H. Whitaker, *Philo*, 10 Vols. and 2 Supplementary Vols., ed. R. Marcus, Loeb Classical Library, London & Cambridge, Mass.: Heinemann & Harvard, 1929–1962.

Sefer Harazim:

Margalioth, M., *Sefer Harazim*, Jerusalem: American Academy for Jewish Research, 1966.

4. HELLENISTIC RELIGION AND CULTURE AND THEIR RELATION TO JUDAISM

Cumont, F., *Oriental Religions in Roman Paganism*, Chicago: Open Court, 1911.

Dodds, E. R., *The Greeks and the Irrational*, Berkeley: Univ. of California, 1959.

Festugière, A.-M., *Personal Religion among the Greeks*, Berkeley: Univ. of California, 1954.

*Fischel, H. A., "Studies in Cynicism and the Ancient Near East: The Transformation of a *Chria*", *Religions in Antiquity (E. R. Goodenough Memorial)*, ed. J. Neusner, *Numen Suppl.* 14 (1968) 372–411.

Goodenough, E. R., *An Introduction to Philo Judaeus*, New Haven: Yale, 1940.

Goodenough, E. R., *Jewish Symbols in the Greco-Roman Period*, New York: Pantheon, 1953–1968, 13 vols.

Liebermann, S., *Greek in Jewish Palestine*, New York: Jewish Theological Seminary, 1950.

Liebermann, S., *Hellenism in Jewish Palestine*, New York: Jewish Theological Seminary, 1962.

Weitzmann, K., *Studies in Classical and Byzantine Manuscript Illumination*, Chicago: Univ. of Chicago, 1971.

5. THE THIRD CENTURY, APOCALYPSES AND ESCHATOLOGY

Collins, J. J., *The Apocalyptic Vision of the Book of Daniel*, Harvard Semitic Monographs 16, Missoula: Scholars Press, 1977.

*Cross, F. M., Jr., "A Reconstruction of the Judaean Restoration" *Journal of Biblical Literature* 94 (1975) 4–18.

*Greenfield, J. C. & Stone, M. E., "The Enochic Pentateuch and the Date of the Similitudes" *Harvard Theological Review* (1977) (forthcoming).

Hanson, P. D., *The Dawn of Apocalyptic*, Philadelphia: Fortress, 1975.

Koch, K., *The Rediscovery of Apocalyptic*, London: SCM, 1972.

Milik, J. T., *The Books of Enoch*, Oxford: 1976 (see as to this The Key to Ancient Writings, under Enoch, Book of, *infra*).

Nickelsburg, G. W. E., *Resurrection, Immortality and Eternal Life in Intertestamental Judaism*, Harvard Theological Studies 26; Cambridge, Mass., Harvard, 1972.

Russell, D. S., *The Method and Message of Jewish Apocalyptic*, Philadelphia: Westminster, 1964.

Smith, M., *Palestinian Parties and Politics that Shaped the Old Testament*, New York: Columbia, 1971.

Stone, M. E., "The Book of Enoch and Judaism in the Third Century, B.C.E.", *Catholic Biblical Quarterly* (1978) (forthcoming).

*Stone, M. E., "Lists of Revealed Things in Apocalyptic Literature" *Magnalia Dei (G. E. Wright Memorial)* eds. F. M. Cross Jr., W. Lemke and P. D. Miller, New York: Doubleday, 1976.

6. SECTS AND SCROLLS

Cross, F. M. Jr., *The Ancient Library of Qumrân and Modern Biblical Studies*, New York: Doubleday, 1958.

Finkelstein, L., *The Pharisees*, 2 Vols., Philadelphia: Jewish Publication Society, 1962.

Flusser, D., "The Dead Sea Scrolls and Pre-Pauline Christianity", *Scripta Hierosolymitana* 4 (1958) 215–266.

Kraft, R. A., "The Multiform Jewish Heritage of Early Christianity", *Christianity, Judaism and Other Greco-Roman Cults (M. Smith Festschrift)*, ed. J. Reusner, Leiden: Brill, 1975, 174–199.

Löwenstamm, A., "The Samaritans" *Encyclopaedia Judaica*, Vol. 14, Jerusalem, Keter, 1971, 738–758; cf. 726–730.

Milik, J. T., *Ten Years of Discovery in the Judean Desert*, London: SCM, 1959.

Moore, G. F., *Judaism*, 3 Vols.; Cambridge Mass., Harvard, 1927.

Ringgren, H., *The Faith of Qumrân*, Philadelphia: Fortress, 1963.

Stendahl, K., *The Scrolls and the New Testament*, New York: Harper Bros., 1957.

Stone, M. E., "Judaism at the Time of Christ", *Scientific American* 288 (Jan. 1973) 80–87.

Tcherikover, V., *Hellenistic Civilization and the Jews*, Philadelphia: Jewish Publication Society, 1961.

Urbach, E. E., *The Sages: Their Concepts and Beliefs*, 2 Vols., Jerusalem: Magnes, 1975.

7. GNOSTICISM AND MYSTICISM

Goldin, J., "The Magic of Magic and Superstition", *Aspects of Religious Propaganda in Judaism and Early Christianity*, ed. F. S. Fiorenza, Notre Dame: 1976, 115–147.

Goodenough, E. R., *By Light, Light: The Mystical Gospel of Hellenistic Judaism*, New Haven: Yale, 1940.

Jonas, H., *The Gnostic Religion*, 2 ed., Boston: Beacon, 1963.

*MacRae, G. W., "The Jewish Background of the Gnostic Sophia Myth", *Novum Testamentum* 12 (1970) 86–101.

Nock, A. D., "Greek Magical Papyri", *Essays on Religion and the Ancient World*, ed. Z. Stewart, Oxford: 1972, 1.176–194.

*Pearson, B. A., "Jewish Haggadic Traditions in the *Testimony of Truth* from Nag Hammadi", in *Ex Orbe Religionum (Widengren Festschrift)*, Numen Suppl. 21, Leiden: Brill, 1972, 1.457–470.

Scholem, G. G., *Major Trends in Jewish Mysticism*, New York: Schocken, 1941.

*Scholem, G. G., *Jewish Gnosticism, Merkabah Mysticism and Talmudic Tradition*, 2 ed., New York: Jewish Theological Seminary, 1965.

Key to Ancient Writings

This key provides brief information about each of the ancient writings mentioned in the text above. An acceptable translation is indicated and, if it is in a work included in the Bibliography, then only a short title is given. (In this KEY, "Dead Sea Scrolls translations" refers to the works cited in the preceding Bibliography, Section 3, Primary Sources, under the heading "Dead Sea Scrolls".)

Abraham, Apocalypse of: A Jewish writing presenting a vision seen by Abraham as well as legends about him. It survives only in Old Church Slavonic and was probably written in the second century C.E.
Source: G. H. Box, *The Apocalypse of Abraham*, London: Society for the Promotion of Christian Knowledge (hereafter cited as "SPCK"), 1919.

Adam and Eve, Books of: A number of closely related versions of a writing dealing with the story of the protoplasts. Forms of the book survive in Greek (called *The Apocalypse of Moses*), Latin (*The Life of*

Adam and Eve), Old Church Slavonic (same title), Georgian and Armenian (*The Penitence of Adam*). All of these may derive from a Jewish source document, the language and date of which are unknown.
Source: Charles, *APOT*, 2.

Adam, Apocalypse of: An apparently Sethian gnostic revelation received by Adam and transmitted to Seth. Perhaps first or second century C.E. in date, it occurs in Nag Hammadi Codex 5.
Source: Robinson, *Nag Hammadi Library*.

Against Apion: A refutation by Flavius Josephus of Alexandrian anti-Semitic propaganda. Written in Greek after 94 C.E.
Source: Josephus, Loeb Classical Library, Vol. 1.

Angelic Liturgy (4Q Šir Šab): Texts from the Dead Sea Scrolls which purport to give the songs sung by the angels in heaven in connection with their liturgy. A copy of it was also found at Masada. Presumably it is an Essene composition and it is written in Hebrew. Written before 100 B.C.E.
Sources: Dead Sea Scrolls translations: J. Strugnell, "The Angelic liturgy at Qumrân—4Q Serek Širôt 'Ôlat Haššabbat", *Congress Volume Oxford 1959*, VT Sup 7; Leiden: Brill, 1960, 318–45.

Asaph the Physician, Book of: A collection of diverse, medieval, medical writings. The time and place of composition are unknown, but some parts of the book are quite old. It is written in Hebrew.

Source: No English translation exists; the Hebrew text may be found, edited by S. Muntner, in *Sources for the History of Biology*, ed. S. Bodenheimer, Jerusalem: 1952 (in Hebrew).

Astronomical Book of Enoch: see *Enoch, Book of.*

Baruch, Syriac Apocalypse of: An apocalypse, surviving only in Syriac and Syro-Arabic versions. It was written in the aftermath of the destruction of the Temple by the Romans and is closely related to the *Fourth Book of Ezra.* Its chief subjects are the theological issues raised by the destruction.

Source: Charles, *APOT*, 2.

Ben Sira, Wisdom of: This book is also known as *Sirach* or *Ecclesiasticus*. It embodies the teachings of the sage Jeshua b. Sira, who lived and taught in Jerusalem at the start of the second century B.C.E. Composed in Hebrew, the book survives in fragmentary Hebrew manuscripts from Qumrân, Masada and the Cairo Geniza. The complete text of the Greek translation, made by the author's grandson, is included in the Septuagint.

Source: Any edition of the Apocrypha, and Charles, *APOT*, 1.

Biblical Antiquities: Sometimes also called "Pseudo-Philo", this work tells biblical history from Creation to the monarchy. It is extant only in Latin, although the original was probably Hebrew. It seems to have been written before the destruction of the Temple by the Romans.
Source: M. R. James, *The Biblical Antiquities of Philo*, London: SPCK, 1917.

Chariot Texts: The earliest group of Jewish mystical writings. They use the imagery of Ezekiel, chap. 1, the vision of the heavenly chariot (*merkabah*), to describe the heavenly environs of God. Another type of terminology used by these texts speaks of the heavenly palaces (*hekalot*). The texts stem from the mid-first millennium C.E. and are written in Hebrew.
Sources: see further Scholem, *Trends* and *id.*, *Gnosticism*.

Corpus Hermeticum: A collection of semi-gnostic treatises in Greek, probably from Egypt. They seem to have been written between the second and fourth centuries C.E. and some of them have been found at Nag Hammadi.
Sources: Certain treatises can be found translated in R. M. Grant, *Gnosticism*, New York: Harper, 1961.

Damascus Document: An Essene writing known from the Cairo Geniza and Qumrân fragments. It contains information about the history of the sect and prescriptions for the conduct of communal life. It was written in the second or early first century B.C.E. and is in Hebrew.

Sources: Charles, *APOT*, 2; Dead Sea Scrolls translations.

Enoch, Book of: A compendium of five Jewish apocalypses all of which were composed before the destruction of the Second Temple, viz. *The Book of the Watchers* (chaps. 1–36), the *Similitudes of Enoch* (chaps. 37–71), *The Astronomical Book* (chaps. 72–82), *The Dream Visions* (chaps. 83–90) and *The Epistle of Enoch* (chaps. 91–108). These come from diverse periods and circles, the oldest being the first and third parts. As a whole, the book is found only in Ethiopic, but parts of it have been discovered in Greek and in the Aramaic original (the latter from Qumrân).

Sources: Charles, *APOT*, 2; Milik, *Books of Enoch.*

Enoch, Book of the Secrets of: Also known as *2 Enoch* or *Slavonic Enoch.* A Jewish apocalypse from the time before the destruction of the Temple. It is extant only in Old Church Slavonic and it relates Enoch's ascent through the heavens and the revelations received by him there, as well as the history of the antediluvian generations.

Source: Charles, *APOT*, 2.

Enoch, Dream Visions of: see *Enoch, Book of.*

Enoch, Epistle of: see *Enoch, Book of*.

Ecclesiasticus: see *Ben Sira, Wisdom of*.

Ezra, Fourth Book of: Also known as *2 Esdras*. An apocalypse written after the destruction of the Temple by Titus, probably between 95 and 100 C.E. It deals with the theological problems that arose from the destruction of the Temple. Widely diffused among the Christian churches, it has survived in many versions, but the Greek translation and the Hebrew original have both perished.
Source: Any edition of the Apocrypha, and Charles, *APOT*, 2.

4Q PseudDaniel: Fragmentary writings appertaining to the corpus of Danielic books, found at Qumrân. Certain of these are apocalypses. Written before 100 B.C.E.
Source: J. T. Milik, "Prière de Nabonid et autres écrits d'un cycle de Daniel, fragments de Qumrân 4", *Revue Biblique* 63 (1956) 407–415.

Giants, Book of: A writing associated with the Enoch cycle, relating the deeds of the giants who were born of the union of the "sons of God" and human women (Genesis 6:1–4). It is known from fragments found at Qumrân and was also current among the Manichees, morsels of whose translations of it have also been identified. Written before 100 B.C.E.

Sources: J. T. Milik, "Turfan et Qumrân: Livre des Géants juif et Manichéen", *Tradition und Glaube (Festgabe K. G. Kuhn)*, edd. G. Jeremias *et al.*, Göttingen: Vandenhoeck & Ruprecht, 1971, 117–127; Milik, *Books of Enoch cit. supra* (contains references to earlier literature).

Jeremiah, Epistle of: Short work, originally written in Hebrew, designed to exhort the Jews against idolatry. The Greek translation has survived, together with translations made from it. Probably written in or before first century B.C.E.

Source: Any edition of the Apocrypha, and Charles, *APOT*, 1.

Jewish Antiquities: History of the Jews by Flavius Josephus, published in 93–4 C.E. He wrote the book in Greek, and in the city of Rome.

Source: Josephus, Loeb Classical Library, vols. 4–9.

Jewish War: A history of the revolt of the Jews against the Romans in 68–70 C.E. and of the events which led up to it. It was written by Flavius Josephus and was published between 75 and 79 C.E.

Source: Josephus. Loeb Classical Library, vols. 2–3.

Josephus: See under the names of the various works.

Jubilees, Book of: A retelling and expansion of the biblical history from Creation down to Moses. It is presented as an angelic revelation to Moses on Mt. Sinai. It was originally written in Hebrew early in the second century B.C.E., probably in circles like those from which the Essenes developed somewhat later.
Source: Charles, *APOT*, 2.

Judith, Book of: A story, apparently written in the Maccabean period, relating events which are set in an earlier age. The original was written in Hebrew. Notable for the insights it provides into Jewish piety in the third and second centuries B.C.E.
Source: Any edition of the Apocrypha, and Charles, *APOT*, 1.

Levi, Aramaic Testament of: The last will and testament of Levi, son of Jacob. Known from Aramaic fragments from the Cairo Geniza, fragmentary manuscripts from Qumrân and a partial Greek translation. It contains legal, didactic and narrative elements. Written probably in third century B.C.E.
Source: Charles, *APOT*, 2; J. T. Milik, "Le Testament de Lévi en araméen," *Revue Biblique* 60 (1956) 398–406.

Levi, Greek Testament of: The *Testament of Levi* found in *The Testaments of the Twelve Patriarchs, q.v.*

Lives of the Prophets: A collection of biographical notes relating details of the lives and deeds of various prophets. It is attributed to various Christian notables, particularly Epiphanius of Cyprus. The book circulated widely among Christians and probably reflects Jewish sources. Written in the early centuries of the present era.
Source: C. C. Torrey, *The Lives of the Prophets,* Journal of Biblical Literature Monograph Series 1, Philadelphia: SBL, 1946.

Maccabees, First Book of: A history of the Maccabean revolt, written in Hebrew in circles close to the royal court. It survives in Greek and in translations made from Greek. Written in the late second or first centuries B.C.E.
Source: Any edition of the Apocrypha, and Charles, *APOT,* 1.

Maccabees, Second Book of: A history of the Maccabean revolt. A summary of a five-volume history composed in Greek by Jason of Cyrene. It survives in the original and in translations made from it.
Source: Any edition of the Apocrypha, and Charles, *APOT,* 1. Probably written in the first century B.C.E.

Maccabees, Fourth Book of: A book written in Greek by a Hellenized Jew to show the rule of reason over the passions. The martyrs of the Maccabean revolt serve as his chief examples.
Source: Charles, *APOT,* 2.

Manual of Discipline: see *Order of the Community*.

Merkabah Texts: see *Chariot Texts*.

Midrash of Shemhazai and Azazel: A piece of mediaeval Hebrew legend containing material in the tradition of the fallen angels.
Source: Milik, *Books of Enoch*. Oxford, 1976.

Moses, Testament of: Also known as the *Assumption of Moses*. This writing relates Moses' last charge to Joshua. Its present form dates from early in the first century C.E. but an older writing, of the time of the Maccabean revolt, underlies this. Probably originally written in Hebrew, this work survives only in a single, incomplete Latin manuscript. It contains much important eschatological teaching.
Source: Charles, *APOT*, 2.

Nahum, Commentary on (4QpNah): Essene commentary on the book of the prophet Nahum, interpreting his words as referring to the sect's history. Probably written late in the first century B.C.E.
Source: Dead Sea Scrolls translations.

Noah, Book of: One or more writings which once existed,

attributed to Noah. Fragments and citations alone exist today.

Source: M. R. James, *The Lost Apocrypha of the Old Testament*, London: SPCK, 1920, 11–12; Stone, *Encyclopaedia Judaica*, 12.1198.

On the Contemplative Life: A treatise by Philo of Alexandria (25 B.C.E.–50 C.E.) describing the way of life of the Jewish sect of the Therapeutae in Egypt.
Source: Philo, Loeb Classical Library, vol. 9.

Order of the Community: Also known as the *Manual of Discipline.* An Essene writing found in a number of Qumrân manuscripts. It provides the regulations for the life of the community and is written in Hebrew. It was composed sometime in the late second or early first century B.C.E.
Source: Dead Sea Scrolls translations.

Order of the War: The probable title of the writing also known as *War of the Sons of Light against the Sons of Darkness.* One of the Dead Sea Scrolls which prescribes the form and details of the eschatological battle between the righteous and the wicked. Written in Hebrew.
Source: Dead Sea Scrolls translations.

Poimandres: the first treatise of the *Corpus Hermeticum, q.v.*

Sefer Harazim: A magical work, extant in Hebrew, stemming apparently from the Rabbinic period. It has survived in fragmentary Geniza manuscripts and through re-use in later sources.
Source: No English translation exists. See the study by J. Goldin, "The Magic of Magic and Superstition," *Aspects of Religious Propaganda in Judaism and Early Christianity*, ed. E. S. Fiorenza, Notre Dame: 1976, 115–147.

Sibylline Oracles: Collection of oracles fabricated by Jewish and Christian propagandists over the early centuries C.E. They were attributed to the Sibyl, a pagan prophetess.
Source: Charles, *APOT*, 2.

Similitudes of Enoch: see *Enoch, Book of.*

Solomon, Testament of: A Greek work, Christian in its present form, containing extensive legendary and magical traditions associated with king Solomon.
Source: F. C. Conybeare, "The Testament of Solomon", *Jewish Quarterly Review* 11 (1898) 1–45.

Solomon, Wisdom of: A book of Wisdom teachings attributed to Solomon. It was apparently composed in Greek in Alexandria by a Jewish author about the turn of the era.

Source: Any edition of the Apocrypha, and Charles, *APOT*, 1.

Testimony of Truth: A gnostic treatise from Codex 9 from Nag Hammadi in Egypt. Originally written in Greek, perhaps in Alexandria.
Source: Robinson, *Nag Hammadi Library.*

Tobit, Book of: A story about a Jewish family in the eastern diaspora. The Aramaic original has perished, except for a few fragments, but the book is preserved in full in Greek and in translations made from Greek. It is pre-Christian in date.
Source: Any edition of the Apocrypha, and Charles, *APOT*, 1.

Twelve Patriarchs, Testaments of the: A work giving the last wills and testaments of the twelve sons of Jacob. It survives in Greek in a Christian form but clearly contains many older, Jewish sectarian elements. One of its sources may be the *Aramaic Testament of Levi.* It is important for the study of Jewish ethical and eschatological teaching.
Source: Charles, *APOT*, 2.

War of the Sons of Light against the Sons of Darkness: see *Order of the War.*

Watchers, Book of the: see *Enoch, Book of.*

INDEX